ALL MAJESTY AND POWER

ALL MAJESTY
and
POWER

An Anthology of Royal Prayers

Edited by

DONALD GRAY

William B. Eerdmans Publishing Company
Grand Rapids, Michigan / Cambridge, U.K.

First published 2000 in Great Britain by
Hodder and Stoughton Ltd
A Division of Hodder Headline
338 Euston Road
London NW1 3BH

This edition published 2002 by Wm. B. Eerdmans Publishing Co.
255 Jefferson Ave. S.E., Grand Rapids, Michigan 49503 /
P.O. Box 163, Cambridge CB3 9PU U.K.

Printed in the United States of America

07 06 05 04 03 02   7 6 5 4 3 2 1

Library of Congress Cataloging-in-Publication Data

ISBN 0-8028-3957-6

For the Grandchildren

CONTENTS

ACKNOWLEDGMENTS

I am grateful for the help, advice and invaluable direction to sources received from a number of people during the compilation of this book of prayers.

My particular thanks are due to: The Revd Dr Paul Bradshaw, The Very Revd Mgsr Patrick Byrne, The Revd Alan Gyle, David Hebblethwaite, The Revd Charles Robertson, The Revd Dr Derek Stanesby, The Revd Michael Thompson, Dr Donald Withey, and the libraries at Westminster Abbey and St Paul's Cathedral.

It was Judith Longman at Hodder and Stoughton who first suggested the idea of this book and has been a regular source of encouragement. As always my wife Joyce has battled to produce a typescript from my demanding manuscript.

INTRODUCTION

This collection is in two parts: prayers *for* royalty and prayers *by* royalty. There is a good deal in both Scripture and tradition actively to encourage the former, and diligent search can reveal many interesting and intriguing examples of the latter.

BIDDEN BY THE SCRIPTURES

The Hebrew Scriptures look back to David as the ideal king. He had established his throne at Jerusalem and exercised a wide and weighty rule. In times of adversity the Jews comforted themselves with God's promise to David, 'Your family and your kingdom will be established for ever in my sight; your throne will endure for all time' (2 Samuel 7:16). David prayed that God's continuing blessing might 'rest upon your servant's house for ever'. Yet he and the people were always aware that, as the Psalmist says, 'The Lord is King for ever and ever.'

It is perhaps surprising to realise that during the captivity in Babylon the Jews prayed for the kings of that land. In the sixth century BC, Baruch managed to persuade the Babylonian authorities to return some of the holy vessels which had been looted from the Temple in Jerusalem and he sent them back there with this message:

> The money we are sending you is to be used to buy whole-offerings, sin-offerings, and frankincense, and to provide grain offerings; you are to offer them on the altar of the Lord our God, with prayers for King Nebuchadnezzar of Babylon and for his son Belshazzar, that their life may last as long as the heavens are above the earth. (Baruch 1:10–11)

Then, on their return from Babylon, King Darius issued instructions for the Jews to be provided with the wherewithal to 'offer soothing sacrifices to the God of heaven, and pray for the life of the King and his sons' (Ezra 6:10).

The tension between the need to recognise both God's ultimate authority (and 'kingship') and the rule of a God-given earthly ruler was preserved in the Psalms. In them God's sovereignty is proclaimed, but they also included petitions for the earthly king, notably Psalm 132 which commences, 'Lord, remember David.' So it was that the king prayed for his people, and the people prayed for their ruler. Some of these prayers have been carried over into the Christian era. For the past two hundred years in Westminster Abbey during the anointing, that most solemn moment of the coronation rite, the choir has sung Handel's anthem 'Zadok the Priest . . . anointed Solomon King' with its rousing and unforgettable climax, 'And all the people rejoiced and said, "God save the King! May the King live for ever!" '

In Christian times it has long been argued that prayers for the sovereign are not an optional extra, but a duty laid upon believers. Christians start from an acknowledgment that God's intervention in history, through the incarnation of his Son, has changed for ever both the dignity of humanity and the status of this world. They go on to make the point that a consequence of this God-afforded dignity ought to be a respect for ordered society. By the time that the first letter to Timothy was written, Christians believed that they should pray for all those in positions of authority: 'I urge that petitions, prayers, intercessions, and thanksgivings be offered for everyone, for sovereigns and for all in high office' (1 Timothy 2:1–2).

THE DUTY OF THE CHURCH

We must not forget that when this direction to pray was first current among Christians the rulers were all heathen. The Christians, however, did not believe it should alter matters. In the letter to Titus they were exhorted to remind everyone to be submissive to government and the authorities, and to obey them. Probably the earliest New Testament instruction on this matter was the command, 'Give due honour to everyone: love your fellow Christians, reverence God, honour the emperor' in the first letter of St Peter.

The result was this was taken seriously by the early Christians. Yet they recognised that civic authority was not autonomous, that its task had restrictions. In particular it had the task of ensuring a civic peace in which a pious and moral life was possible. St Clement (*c.* 96) prayed to God that rulers may 'piously administer in peace and mildness the authority granted them by thee'. Tertullian, the African church father (*c.* 160–*c.* 225), was at pains to state that Christians were no danger to the state but were good and useful citizens. Thus he stated:

> We are ever praying for all emperors, that they may have a long life, a secure dominion, a safe home, brave armies, a faithful senate, an upright people, a peaceful world, and whatever may be the wishes of the man and Caesar.

Even times of persecution did not relieve the Church of her responsibilities in this regard, it was believed. Dionysius the Great, a Bishop of Alexandria, writing during the persecutions of Gallus in AD 252 said, 'He chased these holy men who interceded with God for his own peace and health. With them, therefore, he drove away their prayers for himself.'

This care, to pray for both believing and nonbelieving monarchs, was enshrined in the early worship of the Church. The fifth-century *Liturgy of St Mark* contains two opportunities to pray for the emperor, as is the case in a number of Eastern rites.

At the very heart of the eucharistic prayer, the priest prays that God would, 'Guard the kingdom of your servant our orthodox and Christ-loving emperor whom you appointed to rule over the land.' In the *Liturgy of St James*, deriving from the church of Jerusalem and Antioch, the formula is, 'Remember, Lord, our pious emperor, his pious empress: lay hold upon weapon and buckler, and stand up to help him.'

IN THE EAST

Both the *Liturgy of St John Chrysostom* and the *Liturgy of St Basil*, those venerable liturgies which are still in current use in the Orthodox Church, having assimilated older rites, preserve the custom of praying for rulers and those in authority.

They were remembered in the 'diptychs', which are the lists of names of the living and departed for whom special prayer is made. The ruling sovereigns were named in the diptychs of the living, at least the emperor and his consort. There is clear evidence of this from the seventh century. In some manuscripts other members of the imperial family were named. This practice lasted until the end of Byzantium, and even thereafter the imperial naming was preserved in the cases of the local ruler, such as the Russian tsar.

The emperor had originally been crowned in the imperial palace, but by the early seventh century this took place in a church, soon to be established as the patriarchal Great Church of Hagia Sophia, and was accompanied by an elaborate ritual stressing the divine nature of the appointment. Whatever part may have been played by army, senate and people, it was God who placed power in the imperial hands. There was a traditional acclamation, 'God gave you to us. God will guard you.'

IN THE WEST

The Frankish Church under the Merovingian and Carolingian kings between AD 500 and 900 had many of its own liturgical traditions before the adoption of the Roman rite under Charlemagne. Their kings had a duty to defend the faithful from attack, a duty which grew as the assaults of non-Christian Vikings and Arabs multiplied within and around Frankish territory. Then there was a further duty, to extend the boundaries of Christianity, which accounts for the nature of the prayer of the Gallican church: 'Let us pray for the most Christian kings, that our Lord God shall subject all barbarous people to our perpetual peace.'

In those two centuries at the beginning of the second millennium which saw the emergence of much which is characteristic of European culture and religion, all kings, the emperor included, were perceived as God's agents, set apart for government by the anointing which they had received. The anointing of a king could take place only once, but he would show himself many times at a crown-wearing or coronation. At the ceremonies there was a traditional prayer in which the king was seen as the means by which peace and virtue were bestowed upon the people, 'and so may this people thrive under his government and be blessed with eternal life.' It is recorded that at one of William the Conqueror's crown-wearings a spectator fell down, crying out, 'Behold, I see God!'

Up until the sixth century, in the *oratio fidelium*, the prayers of the faithful (or as some prefer 'the universal prayer') of the Latin or Roman eucharistic rites, the most frequently recurring of all themes was prayer for the Church and clergy, and prayer for emperors and kings. In his treatise *On the Sacraments*, St Ambrose gives evidence from Milan in the last quarter of the fourth century to the effect that before the consecration, prayers of intercession were offered for the people, for kings, and for other needs. These prayers which came early in the service did, as many commentators have observed, fulfil the injunction in 1 Timothy to pray 'for all men; for kings and all that are in high places'. However, these prayers disappeared from the regular liturgy in Rome under Pope Gelasius between 492 and 496, to be replaced by a litany which in its turn vanished about a century later. The only trace of the existence of this litany is in the solemn prayers in the liturgy for Good Friday – including a prayer for the emperor. Until modern reforms, the only intercessions were those within the canon of the Mass, which, apart from some regional variations, did not include a prayer for king or emperor.

This was the general situation in Western Christendom at the time of the Reformation. However, England was one of those countries where there existed local variations containing appropriate liturgical provision, but even this was sparse by later standards.

An early exhortation came in 747 when, at the Synod of Cloveshoo (no one is quite sure where in England that was!), it was decreed that:

> henceforth Ecclesiastics and Monastics should in their Canonical Hours entreat the Divine clemency, not only for themselves, but for Kings, Dukes, and for the safety of all Christian people, that they may deserve to lead a quiet and peaceable life under their pious protection.

At the beginning of the canon of the Mass according to the *Sarum Use*, which was the missal most commonly used in England immediately prior to imposition of the *Book of Common Prayer*, God is asked to accept the eucharistic offering on behalf of the Holy Catholic Church together with the pope, the bishop 'and our king' (who was named). There was additionally a *Missa pro rege* for use on suitable occasions.

Incidentally, in later times, while the missal of Pius V (1570) was still in use, by way of special privilege, it was agreed that a monarch might be mentioned in the canon by particular arrangement. Examples of this custom occurred in Spain, and between 1761 and 1918 in the Hapsburg Empire.

THE BEGINNING OF THE ANGLICAN TRADITION

It will come as no surprise to realise that the hands-on involvement of the kings and queens of England in religious affairs in the sixteenth and seventeenth centuries resulted in an expansion of both the time and trouble which was expected to be taken over royal prayers in divine worship.

By the time of Henry VIII there was a tendency for the Church to express its respect for the crown in somewhat fulsome terms. We recall the description of King Henry as 'defender of the faith' justified both by his support of the Roman Church against the French but also by his learned book against Lutheran heresies. In return the clergy reciprocated by the spiritual service of prayers, even for some of the monarch's purely secular actions such as military expeditions. In 1492 Thomas Rotherham, Archbishop of York, issued instructions that his clergy should pray for the king, his army and for the good estate of the realm. In 1513 prayers were ordered for Henry VIII's expedition to the continent. In 1504 the Canterbury Convention laid down a series of prayers to be said for the king during his life, and also promised to say a requiem, in a precisely designated form, after his death.

Continuing evidence of this is the intrusion of a prayer for the king at the beginning of the order for 'The Supper of the Lord and the Holy Communion, Commonly called the Masse' in the first *Book of Common Prayer* authorised during King Edward VI's reign in 1549. The priest was given the opportunity of choice between two prayers. Then later in the service, in the canon of the Mass, the priest prayed for the king that 'under him we may be godly and quietly governed'. Each subsequent revision of the prayer book retained the prayers at the beginning of the service, and by 1662 the later petition for the king (or queen) had become part of the 'Prayer for the Church Militant' which was said at every Holy Communion service. Remarkably Matins and Evensong did not include a prayer for the sovereign for many years – not until the 1662 revision.

The earliest form of the 'Prayer for the King's Majesty', perhaps the best known of all royal prayers, was appended to a new edition of (the by then) late John Fisher's *Psalms and Prayers*, issued in 1544 from the press of Thomas Berthelet (or Bartlett). He was king's printer at the end of the reign of Henry VIII. Although Matins and Evensong in the 1549 prayer book contained the versicle 'O Lord save the King' and its response 'And mercifully hear us when we call upon thee', no other prayer was included; yet the prayer was in the reformed Primer of 1553. Primers had been devotional books for the educated laity, but this version was intended for use in teaching children. In 1559 the prayer was subsequently shortened and placed at the end of the litany, as one of the first liturgical publications of the reign of Elizabeth I.

... AND ALL THE ROYAL FAMILY

The phrase 'and all the royal family' is the catch-all conclusion of the opening of the 'Prayer for the Royal Family', but nonetheless the named individuals and their honours and titles have contained a number of curiosities in the past three hundred or more years.

It was in 1604 that a prayer for the royal family first appeared entitled, 'A Prayer for the Queen and Prince, and other the King and Queen's children'. It was placed at the end of the litany after the 'Prayer for the King'. The prayer provided proved to have its own in-built problems. It commenced with the words,

> Almighty God, which hast promised to be a Father of thine elect and of their seed, we humbly beseech thee to bless our gracious Queen Anne, Prince Henry, and all the King and Queen's royal progeny.

The prayer was republished in 1625 with a change of opening words. It commenced by addressing the

Almighty as 'the fountain of all goodness' for the reason that the sovereign was at that time without issue. In 1632 the delicate phrase was replaced and Prince Charles and the Lady Mary were named in the prayers, but a year later it was again and finally removed; a solution which thus avoided the necessity of continued alteration at this point in the prayer for the royal family.

The sensitivities of who, or who should not, be prayed for in addition to the sovereign had already arisen in the days before a prayer for the royal family had found a place in the prayer book. One of Westminster Abbey's most prized possessions is what is known as the *Lytlington Missal*. The order is based upon the *Sarum Use*. First mentioned in an inventory of 1388, where it is said to have been the gift of Nicholas Lytlington who was Abbot of Westminster from 1362 to 1386, the book not surprisingly did not escape the notice of Henry VIII' investigatory 'visitors'. Along with the numerous expected erasures of the word *papa* there is an intriguing manuscript alteration in the canon of the Mass. At the point where there is a prayer for the king, a middle-sixteenth-century hand has inserted '*Rege nostro H. Regina N*' – the scribe with excellent foresight not venturing to give the initial of the queen's name!

The complication of Henry VIII's marital arrangements was followed by the reign of the boy King Edward VI and then later by the childless reign of Elizabeth I. This meant that it was not until 1604, when England had a king who was both husband and father, that there was a need for a prayer for the royal family. As we have seen, King James I, his queen, and until his early death in 1631, Henry Prince of Wales were the first members of the royal family to be publicly and statutorily the subject of the Church's prayers.

On the restoration of the monarchy in 1660 the prayer book was revised again and the prayers for the king and the royal family were now removed from the position they had previously occupied at the close of the litany and placed in the more familiar place among the final prayers at Matins and Evensong.

The first time the prayer was printed for use in Morning and Evening Prayer in 1662, the list included the widow of the executed King Charles I, who survived until 1699, and was thus prayed for as 'Mary the Queen Mother'. In early forms of the prayer the king's daughters were prayed for in the English style, 'the Lady Elizabeth' or 'the Ladies Mary and Anne' rather than the later Hanoverian, and continental, form of 'Princess'.

Royal prayers were used as a political weapon at the beginning of the eighteenth century. From 1689 until around 1715, in the main, Scottish episcopalians were motivated by Jacobitism. They were unable to accept the Hanoverian succession and believed the House of Stuart should be providing the monarch for both England and Scotland. In 1712 an Act of Parliament provided a shibboleth by which the loyalty of Episcopal ministers could be tested. Legal toleration was to be allowed to those who would not only take oaths to Queen Anne, but also pray for her and the Princess Sophia of Hanover (at that time the heir to the throne) by name in public worship.

Sadly none of Queen Anne's own seventeen children lived long enough to be prayed for by name. In the reign of George II, Frederick Prince of Wales was prayed for until his early death in 1737. It was now the future George III who was heir to the throne, and also Prince of Wales, and his mother enjoyed the unique title of 'Princess Dowager of Wales'. So the prayer book contained, 'their Royal Highnesses George Prince of Wales, the Princess Dowager, the Duke, the Princesses and all the Royal Family'. This was the first time the style 'Royal Highness' had been used in the prayer, but it was later dropped.

George IV took it upon himself personally to forbid the naming of Queen Caroline in the Church's prayers. The king could have claimed a precedence in that when George I arrived from Hanover, Sophia Dorothea was never prayed for as 'our gracious Queen'. During the reign of William IV no heir to the throne was prayed for. It has been suggested that this made a small contribution toward the long deception practised on the Princess Victoria, who did not know for some time how near she stood to the throne.

The title 'Queen Mother' has been carefully preserved in the prayers for those who have been just that – mother of the reigning sovereign. For instance the widow of Queen Victoria's predecessor was known as 'Adelaide the Queen Dowager'. The queen's mother was the Duchess of Kent but, never having been Queen Consort, could not be known as the Queen Mother.

MODERN REVISIONS

In the period from 1662 to the beginning of this century there were, from time to time, proposals to amend or revise the Church's services. Outbreaks of liturgical anarchy in the second half of the nine-teenth century precipitated what would now be almost unthinkable: a government decision to find time and money for no less than a Royal Commission to examine the Church of England's worship. This commission eventually reported that the current law of public worship in the Church of England was 'too narrow for the religious life of the present generation' and that it 'needlessly condemns much which a great section of Church people, including many of her devoted members, value'. So the Royal Com-missioners told the Church to get busy and revise its prayer book. That was in 1902 – the task was not completed until 1980!

Two world wars did not help, but a parliamentary fiasco in 1927 and 1928 added to the confusion. A whole new prayer book had been prepared by the Church, and passed by large majorities by its legislative bodies, but failed to obtain parliamentary approval. It was not for a further thirty years, the Church having obtained more control over its affairs, that an alternative to the *Book of Common Prayer* was fully authorised.

In the 1927/8 proposals, the prayer for the sovereign at the beginning of the Holy Communion service disappeared, but the petitions in the 'prayer for the Church' remained. In the revision of Morning and Evening Prayer it is left to the discretion of the officiant whether to pray for the King's Majesty. The book provides a collection of fifty-eight prayers and thanksgivings from which to choose. As well as the prayer from the Holy Communion for the king this section includes those for both the king and the royal family from Morning and Evening Prayer. A new composition, subsequently often used, 'For the King and all in authority under him', appeared for the first time in the proposed book.

In the years following the disaster of the parliamentary rejection of that revised book, many manuals of suitable prayers were produced as a result of both commercial endeavour and lay and clerical enthusiasm. The title of one of the most widely used aptly described their purpose: *After the Third Collect*. This private enterprise is the source of many of the prayers which follow in this collection.

Before leaving the official Church of England books, however, we must cast an eye over *The Alternative Service Book 1980* – the result of that long-delayed process of liturgical revision. It continues the custom of its ill-fated predecessor and leaves decisions regarding the content of prayers, after the collects, at Morning and Evening Prayer to the officiant. By the time the *ASB* appeared, private compilations had so overtaken events it was not thought necessary to include more than a basic minimum of possible prayers. Just six prayers of intercession, thanksgiving and dedication are provided. These include the 'Prayer for the Queen and all in authority under her', and one for the royal family. In the suggested pattern given for the 'Prayer for the Church' in the Order for the Holy Communion the form, 'Bless and guide Elizabeth our Queen' is included.

The permissive nature of these provisions has, from time to time, been the subject of speeches of criticism by more traditionally minded members of the General Synod of the Church of England. The apparent laxity of the rubrics of *The Alternative Service Book 1980* on this matter has also provided an amount of correspondence both to the archbishops and to the Liturgical Commission which has the task of preparing texts of services for the General Synod's consideration. The commission has, in its recent proposals, responded by ensuring that the state prayers have an appropriate prominence in services and the archbishops have made it clear to correspondents that they believe both the Queen and her family ought to be regular subjects of the Church's prayers.

WHY PRAY?

The idea of intercessory prayers creates problems even for some of the most devout believers. How can God hear each and every prayer that is being offered at one and the same time? Surely some of those prayers and petitions are in many ways contradictory and will only serve to cancel each other out? Of course intercession is an act of faith and trust, and is usually a work for others. By such prayer we make an act of faith in God, his caring, his goodness. The whole business is involved, we realise, in the mystery of God and the freedom of humanity. We make bold to intercede for others because of what we fundamentally believe about God as our loving Father, who works directly, but also through men and women, using their co-operation. In the end, intercession depends upon a life of faith, not in words.

With that in mind, how often ought we to pray for the Queen and how effective will it be? Sir Francis Galton (1822–1911), the polymath who was at one and the same time scientist, inventor, explorer and statistician, and who pioneered the study of eugenics, thought he ought to try and evaluate the efficiency of intercessory prayer. For such a study he decided that royalty were a suitable subject being (certainly in his day) among those most persistently and regularly prayed for. His researches into the mortality statistics of royalty did not reveal a high level of effectiveness. He discovered that there appeared to be no discernible beneficial results. In fact, Galton alleged that he discovered that royal personages, on the whole, did not live as long as other folk! Such scepticism, however, was not able to quantify the benefits of prayer on the sovereign's inclination to serve the will of God, and their work in preserving the people in wealth, peace and godliness.

Even among the royal family there have been times when it was believed that the constant repetition of prayer was not necessarily the best way of serving queen and country. In one of her regular letters home Sarah, Lady Lyttleton, who was governess to Queen Victoria's eldest children between 1842 and 1850, recorded the following conversation. It took place during the time of the Queen's first pregnancy between a certain 'Lord W' and the Queen's husband, Prince Albert.

> *Lord W* asked if a prayer for the Queen's peculiar circumstances should be added [to the liturgy].
> *Prince* – No, no, you have one already in the litany for 'all women labouring with child'. You already pray five times for the Queen. It is too much.
> *Lord W* – Can we pray too much for her Majesty?
> *Prince* – Not too *heartily* but too *often*.

There is also an example of Queen Victoria being the subject of misdirected prayer. St Kilda, the archipelago which lies 110 miles to the west of the Scottish mainland, was often isolated by both distance and the fury of north Atlantic storms. In 1836, after St Kilda had been completely cut off for two years, the minister found, when a passing ship dropped anchor in Village Bay, that he had been praying for King William several months after his death. He immediately changed his prayers to 'His Majesty' and it was not until the spring of 1838, when Queen Victoria had been on the throne for nearly a year, that to his embarrassment he finally learned the sex of the new monarch.

NOT JUST THE CHURCH OF ENGLAND

If, so far, when considering modern and contemporary prayer for the Queen and the royal family we seemed to have concentrated on the established Church of England, that is not to suggest that the other Christian churches in Britain do not pray for them. There was a long tradition in the Roman Catholic Church to pray for the sovereign after the main Mass on a Sunday. Sadly this does not seem to happen often these days. Where the Queen, and perhaps more rarely, the royal family might be prayed for in the average Roman Catholic parish on a Sunday is within the general intercession which is part of every Mass. The modern Roman Catholic service book does contain prayers, and examples are included in this collection but, as in the present-day

Church of England services, there is a good deal of what can only be called 'pot luck' involved. This haphazard observance of the custom of praying for the Queen would seem to be the current situation in all the mainstream Christian churches.

PRAYERS NORTH OF THE BORDER

It should be acknowledged that the Church of Scotland has always been particularly careful to include the opportunity to pray for the Queen especially in its official formularies, but it is well known that the water, the horse and its thirst are often three different programmes.

Prayers for the ruling monarch have often caused problems in Scotland. For instance during the Civil War, the Cromwellian government in Scotland decreed that all ministers who prayed for King Charles I would be expelled. An anonymous minister wrote to the King's son to tell him of this, and claimed he had found a way round the ban, and that he and his friends intended:

> to forbear the word King in prayer, yet so as to pray in such terms as the people who observe might find where to put in their shoulder and bear you up in public prayer. As thus, 'Lord, remember in mercy every distressed person and every distressed family: and the lower their condition be, and from how much the higher

station they are laid low, so much the more now
remember them in mercy and let us not be
guilty, as they who remember not the afflictions
of Joseph: but remember David, Lord, in all his
troubles' or to this effect: so that you see the
duty is done in effect, the people understand it,
and are discerned to join their sighs and groans,
although the word of degree (*the word of rank,
i.e. 'King'*) be not used.

The Reverend John Lumsden, Minister of Canon-
gate, was deprived of his ecclesiastical office by the
Privy Council for refusing to read the proclamation
for the Estates and for not praying for the new King
and Queen, William and Mary, in 1689. Instead,
he had prayed for King James VII (James II of
England), in his view still the rightful king in spite
of the Revolution Settlement, that God 'would give
him the necks of his enemies and the hearts of his
subjects'.

After his victory at Prestonpans in 1745, Prince
Charles resided for a while in Holyrood Palace.
He prohibited all rejoicings for the victory, on the
grounds that the losers were also his father's subjects.
He exhorted the ministers of Edinburgh to resume
their duties, now that the city was quiet again. They
sent a deputation to know whether they would be
permitted to pray for King George. The Prince
could not give them permission, as to do so would
be to give the lie to his father's claims; but he indi-
cated that he would not call them to account for any

imprudent language they might use in their public prayers.

On the Sunday following, the Minister of St Cuthbert's, Mr MacVicar, took advantage of this, and prayed for King George, 'stoutly asserting his right to the throne'. Some Jacobites in the congregation thought this was excessive and complained to the Prince, who declined to interfere. Next Sunday, Mr MacVicar again prayed for King George, but added, 'As to this young person (*Prince Charles*) who has come among us seeking an earthly crown, do Thou, in Thy merciful favour, give him a heavenly one'.

Finally, there is a story that Dr Alexander Whyte of Free St George's, Edinburgh, in the course of the intercessions at Sunday morning service towards the end of the nineteenth century prayed that 'the Queen might be converted'. A correspondence ensued in the columns of *The Scotsman* as to whether this prayer for such a well-loved, morally upright, spiritually alert monarch as Queen Victoria breached decorum if not decency. Much was said about the infelicity of the expression and the inappropriateness of the petition, especially when uttered in a crowded church at a public service. Dr Whyte eventually (and probably gleefully!) joined the fray, and wrote to the newspaper, asking someone to point out to him what precisely was the difference in meaning between asking God to save the Queen, which we prayed every time the National Anthem was sung, and asking God to convert the Queen!

TODAY'S INTERCESSIONS

Attendance at services in any of our churches these days will assure us that there is a great desire to pray for current needs and necessities. Indeed the Sunday morning intercessions can become a cross between the news headlines and the bulletin board. 'You heard it here first', seems sometimes to be the motto. The great disasters, human pain and poverty that assault us through the media are often skilfully packaged for our prayers. If occasionally this is done at too great a length, with a hint of self-regard which seems to be anxious not only to afford the Almighty information, but also suggesting the solution he might provide, that might be the price we have to pay for having rid ourselves of anodyne generalisations and what were often essentially church-orientated requests. What is sad is that too few of our worthy intercessors have a sufficient sense of history and knowledge of our constitution to realise that a prayer for the Queen would be highly appropriate on many occasions.

PARLIAMENTARY CUSTOM

One of the occasions at which a prayer for the Queen is regularly and faithfully afforded is at the daily commencement of business in Parliament at Westminster. Both the House of Commons and the House of Lords have a short form of prayer before their daily work. This does not happen in any side room or chapel but in the parliamentary chambers. In the very House of Commons prayer is conducted by the Speaker's Chaplain, kneeling side by side with the Speaker at the same table at which those dispatch boxes lie from which the principal politicians from each side of the House confront and harangue each other. That the original location of the Commons' chamber was the Palace of Westminster's Chapel takes nothing away from the occasion. In the House of Lords the prayers are normally conducted by the 'duty bishop' – one of the twenty-six diocesan bishops who are members of the Upper House and are organised by rota from Lambeth Palace to undertake this task in 'their Lordships' House'.

Until quite recently the form of prayer used in both Houses has been that which has come down, almost entirely unchanged, from 1661. The only minor changes have been that the House of Lords gives the bishop the choice of a number of psalms (while the Commons Chaplain is still stuck with Psalm 67) and in recent years the corporate recitation of 'the Grace' at the end of the Commons' prayers. However, when the Commons returned after the summer recess in 1998, they found that the Speaker (the Rt Hon. Betty Boothroyd MP) had authorised some 'invisible mending' to be done on the form of prayers, in particular in the royal prayers. In the first place, the prayer for the Queen had been modified, notably by omitting any reference to asking God to preserve her in 'health and wealth'. Many felt that in the light of the Queen's

own known concern about the Civil List and her
willingness to pay taxes, that any petition that seemed
to suggest that God's aid might be invoked to assist
the royal accumulation of riches was, at the best,
insensitive.

The second significant change in the Commons'
prayers has been to omit the prayer for the royal
family. This was not done with any dismissive intent,
but to recognise that they play no part within the
constitutional, parliamentary and legislative life of
the nation. By so doing this change sought to empha-
sise that, within the framework of our constitutional
monarchy, the Queen has a unique and pivotal role
and therefore certainly ought to be included in any
prayers that Parliament prays before its daily session.
At the time of writing although it has been resolved
that sessions of the Scottish Parliament will open with
prayers, the content of those intercessions have not
yet been decided. At present the Welsh Assembly,
surprisingly, seems to have set its face against any
official act of worship before commencing deliberations.

What, one may well ponder, might be the sovereign's own view of such prayers on her behalf
offered in church, chapel or parliamentary chamber.
Clearly she is a devout and thoughtful Christian.
Further I am given to understand that our present
Queen, being herself completely mindful of the need
to pray, and indeed to be prayed for, has expressed
the opinion that, in general, she has no particular
views about *how* she should be prayed for – as long as

she *is* indeed the subject of our prayers. I believe it is both the duty and the responsibility of those of us who pray to do just that – to pray for the Queen.

Prayers by
Royalty

Charles, King and Martyr

O Lord,
   make thy way
   plain before me.

Let thy glory
   be my end,
   thy word my rule;

And then, thy will
   be done.

THE HEBREW SCRIPTURES

In the Bible words of prayer are often put into the mouth of kings. These are some examples from the Old Testament and the Apocrypha.

1

KING DAVID'S PRAYER (2 Samuel 7:18–29)

Who am I, Lord God, and what is my family, that you have brought me thus far? It was a small thing in your sight, Lord God, to have planned for your servant's house in days long past. What more can I say? Lord God, you yourself know your servant David. For the sake of your promise and in accordance with your purpose you have done all this great thing to reveal it to your servant.

Lord God, you are great. There is none like you; there is no God but you, as everything we have heard bears witness. And your people Israel, to whom can they be compared? Is there any other nation on earth whom you, God, have set out to redeem from slavery to be your people? You have won renown for yourself by great and awesome deeds, driving out other nations and their gods to make way for your people whom you redeemed from Egypt. You have established your people Israel as your own for ever, and you, Lord, have become their God.

Now, Lord God, perform for all time what you have promised for your servant and his house; make good what you have promised. May your fame be great for evermore, and let people say, 'The Lord of Hosts is God over Israel'; and may the house of your servant David be established before you. Lord God of Hosts, God of Israel, you have shown me your purpose, in saying to your servant, 'I shall build up your house'; and therefore I have made bold to offer this prayer to you. Now, Lord God, you are God and your promises will come true; you have made these noble promises to your servant. Be pleased now to bless your servant's house so that it may continue always before you; you, Lord God, have promised, and may your blessing rest on your servant's house for ever.

2

A PSALM OF DAVID (Psalm 21)

Lord, the king rejoices in your might:
    well may he exult in your victory.
You have granted him his heart's desire
    and have not refused what he requested.
You welcome him with blessings and prosperity
    and place a crown of finest gold on his head.
He asked of you life, and you gave it to him,

length of days for ever and ever.
Your victory has brought him great glory;
   you invest him with majesty and honour,
for you bestow everlasting blessings on him,
   and make him glad with the joy of your presence,
for the king puts his trust in the Lord;
    the loving care of the Most High keeps him
    unshaken.
Your hand will reach all your enemies,
   your right hand all who hate you;
at your coming you will set them in a fiery furnace;
    in his anger the Lord will engulf them,
    and fire will consume them.
It will destroy their offspring from the earth
   and rid mankind of their posterity.
For they have aimed wicked blows at you;
   in spite of their plots they could not prevail;
but you will aim at their faces with your bows
   and force them to turn in flight.
Be exalted, Lord, in your might;
   we shall sing a psalm of praise to your power.

3

KING SOLOMON'S PRAYER (1 Kings 3:7–9)

Now, Lord my God, you have made your servant king
in place of my father David, though I am a mere child,
unskilled in leadership. Here I am in the midst of

your people, the people of your choice, too many
to be numbered, or counted. Grant your servant,
therefore, a heart with skill to listen so that he may
govern your people justly and distinguish good from
evil. Otherwise who is equal to the task of governing
this great people of yours?

4

KING HEZEKIAH'S PRAYER (Isaiah 37:16–20)

Lord of Hosts, God of Israel, enthroned on the
cherubim, you alone are God of all the kingdoms of
the world; you made heaven and earth. Incline your
ear, Lord, and listen; open your eyes, Lord, and see;
hear all the words that Sennacherib has sent to taunt
the living God. Lord, it is true that the kings of
Assyria have laid waste every country, and have con-
signed their gods to the flames. They destroyed
them, because they were no gods but the work of
men's hands, mere wood and stone. Now, Lord our
God, save us from his power, so that all the kingdoms
of the earth may know that you alone, Lord, are God.

5

KING MANASSEH'S PRAYER

Almighty Lord,
God of our fathers,
   of Abraham, Isaac, and Jacob, and of their
   righteous posterity,
who made heaven and earth in their
   manifold array,
who fettered the ocean by your word
   of command,
who closed the abyss
   and sealed it with your fearful and glorious
   name –
before your power all things quake and tremble.
The majesty of your glory is more than can be
   borne;
none can endure the threat of your wrath against
   sinners.

Your promised mercy is beyond
   measure and none can fathom it;
for you are Lord Most High,
compassionate, patient, and of great mercy,
relenting when men suffer for their sins:
Therefore, Lord God of the righteous,
you appointed repentance not for Abraham, Isaac,
   and Jacob,
who were righteous and did not sin against you,
but for me, whose sins outnumber the

sands of the sea.
My transgressions abound, Lord, my
    transgressions abound,
and, because of the multitude of my
    wrongdoings,
I am not worthy to look up and gaze
    at the height of heaven.
Bowed down with many an iron
    chain,
I grieve over my sins and find no
    relief,
because I have provoked your anger
    and done what is wrong in your eyes,
setting up idols and so multiplying
    offences.

Now my heart submits to you,
    imploring your great goodness.
I have sinned, Lord, I have sinned,
and I acknowledge my transgressions.
I beg and beseech you,
spare me, Lord, spare me;
destroy me not with my transgressions on my
    head,
do not be angry with me for ever,
or store up punishment for me.
Do not condemn me to the depths of the earth,
for you, Lord, are the God of the penitent.
You will show your goodness towards me,
for, unworthy as I am, you will save me in your
    great mercy;

and I shall praise you continually all the
    days of my life.
The whole host of heaven sings your
    praise,
and yours is the glory for ever. Amen.

CONSTANTINE THE GREAT
(*c*. 274–337)

6

O Christ, Ruler and Lord of the world, to Thee we
consecrate this land, its sceptre and its power. Guard
Thy land, guard it from every foe. Amen.

ALFRED THE GREAT (849–99)

7

O Thou Who art the Father of that Son which hast
awakened us, and yet urgest us out of the sleep of
our sins, and exhortest us that we become Thine, to
Thee, Lord, we pray, Who art the supreme Truth,
for all truth that is, is from Thee. Thee we implore,

O Lord, Who art the highest Wisdom, through Thee
are wise, all those that are so. Thou art the supreme
Joy, and from Thee all have become happy that are
so. Thou art the highest Good, and from Thee all
beauty springs. Thou art the intellectual Light, and
from Thee man derives his understanding. To
Thee, O God, we call and speak. Hear us, O Lord,
for Thou art our God and our Lord, our Father and
our Creator, our Ruler and our Hope, our Wealth
and our Honour, our Home, our Country, our Salvation, and our Life; hear, hear us, O Lord. Few of Thy
servants comprehend Thee, but at least we love Thee
– yea, love Thee above all other things. We seek Thee,
we follow Thee, we are ready to serve Thee; under
Thy power we desire to abide, for Thou art the Sovereign of all. We pray Thee to command us as Thou
wilt; through Jesus Christ Thy Son our Lord. Amen.

8

Lord God Almighty,
I pray thee for thy great mercy and by the token of
    the holy rood,
Guide me to thy will, to my soul's need, better than
    I can myself;
And shield me against my foes, seen and unseen;
And teach me to do thy will
        that I may inwardly love thee before all things
        with a clean mind and a clean body.
For thou art my maker and my redeemer,

my help, my comfort, my trust, and my hope.
Praise and glory be to thee now, ever and ever,
world without end.

CANUTE (OR SVEINSSON KNUT)
(994?–1035)

9

May God of His goodness and love keep me King on
my throne in honour. Amen.

HENRY VI (1421–71)

10

Lord Jhesu Crist, that madest me,
That boughtest me on rode-tree
And fore-ordeinedst that I be,
Thou knowst what Thou wouldst do with me;
Do with me now as pleseth Thee.
Amen, Jhesu, for Thy pyte.

11

A 'modernisation' of the above.

O Lord Jesu Christ, who hast made me and redeemed me and brought me where I am upon my way: thou knowest what thou wouldst do with me; do with me according to thy will, for thy tender mercies' sake.

HENRY VIII (1491–1547)

12

A Night Prayer

O Lord, the Maker of all things, we pray Thee now in this evening hour, to defend us through Thy mercy from all deceit of our enemy. Let us not be deluded with dreams, but if we lie awake keep Thou our hearts. Grant this petition, O Father, to Whom with the Holy Ghost, always in heaven and earth, be all laud, praise and honour. Amen.

13

Attributed to 'The Household of Henry VIII' but perhaps by the king himself.

O Almighty God, who hast prepared everlasting life to all those that be thy faithful servants: Grant unto us sure hope of the life everlasting, that we, being in this world, may have some foretaste thereof in our hearts: not by our deserving, but by the merits of our Saviour and Lord Jesu Christ.

EDWARD VI (1547–53)

14

Adapted from 'the Letter Missive which the right noble Prince Edward the Sixt sent to the Kings, Princes, and other Potentates, inhabiting the Northwest partes of the worlde, toward the mighty Empire of Cathay, at such time as Sir Hugh Willoughby, knight, and Richard Chancelor with their company attempted the voyage thither in the yeere of Christ 1553'.

O God of heaven and earth, that providest greatly for mankind and wouldest not that all things should be found in one region, to the end that one should have need of another: We beseech thee bring it to pass that by the friendly means and free passage of trade, searching and carrying both over the land and the sea, friendship may be established among all men, and everyone seek to gratify all, to their own mutual benefits and peace, and to thy glory, which never shall have an end.

15

Preface to Geneva Bible. Sometimes attributed to King Edward VI.

O gracious God and most merciful Father, who hast vouchsafed us the rich and precious jewel of thy holy word: Assist us with thy Spirit that it may be written in our hearts to our everlasting comfort, to reform us, to renew us according to thine own image, to build us up and edify us into the perfect building of thy Christ, sanctifying and increasing in us all heavenly virtues. Grant this, O heavenly Father, for the same Jesus Christ's sake.

QUEEN MARY I (1516–58)

16

Adapted from the Latin of Thomas Aquinas, and in a large degree translated into English by Queen Mary, at the age of eleven.

O merciful God, grant me to covet with a fervent mind those things which truly please thee, to search them wisely, to know them truly, and to fulfil them perfectly, to the laud and glory of thy Name.

Let that labour delight me, which is for thee, and let all the rest weary me, which is not in thee. My most loving Lord and God, give me a waking heart, that no curious thought withdraw me from thee; let it be so strong, that no unworthy affliction draw me backward; so stable, that no tribulation break it. Grant me understanding to know thee, diligence to seek thee, a way of life to please thee, and, finally, hope to embrace thee:

for the sake of our only Saviour, Jesu Christ.

LADY JANE GRAY (1537–54)

17

Merciful God, be thou now unto us a strong tower of defence. Give us grace to await thy leisure, and patiently to bear what thou doest unto us, nothing doubting thy goodness towards us. Therefore do with us in all things as thou wilt: Only arm us, we beseech thee, with thy armour, that we may stand fast; above all things taking to us the shield of faith, praying always that we may refer ourselves wholly to thy will, being assuredly persuaded that all thou doest cannot but be well. And unto thee be all honour and glory.

MARY QUEEN OF SCOTS (1542–87)

18

Written just before her execution.

> O Domine Deus! speravi in te;
> O care mi Jesu! nunc libera me;
> In dura catena, in misera poena,
>   Desidero te.
> Languendo, querendo, et genuflectendo
> Adoro, imploro, ut liberes me!

A translation of Queen Mary's prayer above.

O Lord my God, I hope in thee;
My dear Lord Jesus, set me free;
In chains, in pains,
I long for thee.
On bended knee
I adore thee, implore thee
To set me free.

QUEEN ELIZABETH I (1533–1603)

19

Prayer before her coronation in 1559. 'Her highness, being placed in her chariot within the Tower of London, lifted up her eyes to heaven, and said':

O Lord almighty, and everlasting God, I give thee most hearty thanks, that thou hast been so merciful unto me, as to spare me to behold this joyful day. And I knowledge, that thou hast dealt as wonderfully with me, as thou didst with thy true and faithful servant Daniel the prophet, whom thou deliveredst out of the den, from the cruelty of the greedy raging Lions: even so was I overwhelmed, and only by thee delivered. To thee therefore be only thanks, honour and praise for ever. Amen.

20

Adapted from a prayer composed and said by Queen Elizabeth, after a progress, on 15 August 1574, being then at Bristol.

I render unto Thee (O mercifull and heavenly Father) most humble and hearty thanks for thy manifold mercies so abundantly bestowed upon me, as well for my creation, preservation, regeneration, and all other thy benefites and great mercies exhibited in Christ Jesus, but especially for thy mightie protection and defence over me, in preserving me in this long and dangerous journey, as also from the beginning of my life unto this present hower, from all such perills as I should most justly have fallen into for mine offences, haddest Thou not, O Lord God, of thy great goodness and mercy preserved and kept me. Continue this thy favorable goodness toward me, I beseech Thee, that I may still likewise be defended from all adversity both bodily and ghostly: but specially, O Lord, keep me in the soundness of thy faith, fear, and love, that I never fall away from Thee, but continue in thy service all the daies of my life. Stretch forth, O Lord most mightie, thy right hand over me, and defend me from mine enemys, that they never prevayle against me. Give me, O Lord, the assistance of thy Spiritt, and comfort of thy Grace, truly to know Thee, intirely to love Thee, and assuredly to trust in Thee. And that as I do acknowledge to have received the Government of this Church and Kingdome at thy hand, and to hold the same of Thee, so graunt me grace, O Lord, that in the end I may render up and present the same unto Thee, a peaceable, quiett, and well ordered State and kingdome, as also a perfect reformed Church, to the furtherance of thy Glory. And to my subjects, O Lord God, graunt, I beseech Thee, faithfull and obedient hearts, willingly to submit themselves to the obedience of thy Word and Commandments, that we altogether being thankfull unto Thee for thy benefitts received, may laud and magnifie thy Holy Name world without end. Graunt this, O mercifull Father, for Jesus Christes sake our only Mediatour and Advocate. Amen.

21

Prayer of Queen Elizabeth before the Armada, 1588.

We do instantly beseech Thee of Thy gracious goodness to be merciful to the Church militant here upon earth, and at this time compassed about with most strong and subtle adversaries.

O! let Thine enemies know that Thou hast received England, which they most of all for Thy Gospel's sake do malign, into Thine own protection. Set a wall about it, O Lord, and evermore mightily defend it. Let it be a comfort to the afflicted, a help to the oppressed, and a defence to Thy Church and people persecuted abroad. And, forasmuch as this cause is now in hand, direct and go before our armies, both by sea and land.

Bless them and prosper them, and grant unto them honourable success and victory.

Thou art our help and shield. O! give good and prosperous success to all those that fight this battle against the enemies of Thy Gospel.

22

From a prayer composed by Queen Elizabeth, at the departure of the fleet, 1596.

Most omnipotent, maker and guider of all, who alone searchest and fathomest our hearts, and dost truly discern that no malice of revenge, nor desire of bloodshed, nor greed of gain, hath bred our resolution: Prosper the work we humbly beseech thee, guide the journey, speed the victory, and make the return the advancement of thy glory, and safety of this realm. To these devout petitions, Lord, give thou thy blessed grant.

KING CHARLES I (1600–49)

23

Almighty and most merciful Father, look down upon us, Thy unworthy servants, who here prostrate ourselves at the footstool of Thy throne of grace. Look upon us, O Father, through the mediation and in the merits of Jesus Christ, in Whom only Thou art well pleased, for of ourselves we are not worthy to stand before Thee. As in sin we were born, so we have broken Thy commandments, by thought, words, and works. We confess, O Lord, that it is Thy mercy which endureth for ever. Thy compassion which never fails, which is the cause that we have not been consumed. With Thee there is mercy and plenteous redemption: in the multitude of Thy mercies and by the merits of Jesus Christ, enter not into judgment with Thy servants, but be Thou merciful unto us, and wash away all our sins with that precious blood which our Saviour shed for us. Purify our hearts by Thy Holy Spirit, and as Thou dost add days to our lives, so good Lord, we beseech Thee, to add repentance to our days, that when we have passed this mortal life we may be partakers of Thine everlasting Kingdom; through the merits of Jesus Christ our Lord. Amen.

24

From *Eikon Basilike*, purported to be the meditations of Charles I, and long so regarded; it was published about the date of his execution in 1649.

O Lord, the Governor of all things, set bounds to our passions, to our errors by truth, to our discontents by good laws justly executed, and to our divisions by charity, that we may be, as thy Jerusalem, a country at unity in itself. Grant this, O God, in thy good time and for ever, for Christ's sake.

QUEEN ANNE (1665–1714)

25

Almighty and Eternal God, the Disposer of all the affairs in the world, there is not one circumstance so great as not to be subject to Thy power, nor so small but it comes within Thy care; Thy goodness and wisdom show themselves through all Thy works, and Thy loving-kindness and mercy appear in the several dispensations of Thy Providence. May we readily submit ourselves to Thy pleasure and sincerely resign our wills to Thine, with all patience, meekness, and humility; through Jesus Christ our Lord. Amen.

PRINCESS ELIZABETH (1770–1840)

26

What will befall us to-day, O God, we know not;
we only know that nothing will happen which
Thou hast not foreseen, determined, desired, and
ordered – that is enough for us. Thee do we worship
and adore. We ask in the Name of Jesus Christ our
Saviour, and through His infinite merits, patience in
all our sufferings, perfect submission to Thee for all
that Thou desirest or permittest, guidance in all that
we undertake; for Thine honour and glory we ask it.
Amen.

HRH THE PRINCE PHILIP, DUKE OF EDINBURGH (1921–)

27

O Lord, the Creator of the Universe and author of
the laws of nature, inspire in us thy servants the will
to ensure the survival of all the species of animals

and plants which you have given to share the planet with us.

Help us to understand that we have a responsibility for them and that having dominion does not mean that you have given us the right to exploit the living world without thought for the consequences.

Through him who taught us that Solomon in all his glory could not compete with the flowers in the field.

Prayers for Royalty

Of Prayer for the King

Charles Wheatly, *A Rational Illustration of the Book of Common Prayer of the Church of England, 1720*

We have been hitherto only praying for ourselves; but since we are commanded to *pray for all men*, we now proceed, in obedience to that command, to pray for the whole church; and in the first place for the king, whom, under Christ, we acknowledge to be the supreme governor of this part of it to which we belong. And since the supreme King of all the world is God, for whom all mortal kings reign; and since his authority sets them up, and his power only can defend them; therefore all mankind, as it were by common consent, have agreed to pray to God for their rulers. The heathens offered sacrifices, prayers, and vows for their welfare: and the Jews (as we see by the Psalms) always made their prayers for the king a part of their public devotion. And all the ancient fathers, liturgies, and councils fully evidence, that the same was done daily by Christians, they particularly named them in their offices, with titles expressing the dearest affection, and most honourable respect; and prayed for them in loyal and hearty terms.

FROM APOSTOLIC AND POST-APOSTOLIC TIMES

28

BASED ON 1 TIMOTHY 2:1–3

O God, you have taught us through your servant the apostle Paul to offer prayers and intercessions for sovereigns and all in high office; look with mercy upon all for whom we are bidden to pray, that under your governance we may lead tranquil and quiet lives, free to practise our religion with dignity; through Jesus Christ our Lord. Amen.

29

ST CLEMENT OF ROME (*c.* 95)

Grant unto all Kings and Rulers, O Lord, health, peace, concord, and stability, that they may administer the government which Thou hast given them without failure. For Thou, O heavenly Master, King of the Ages, givest to the sons of men glory and honour, and power over all things that are upon the earth. Do Thou, Lord, direct their counsel according to that which is good and well pleasing in Thy sight, that administering in peace and gentleness, with godliness, the power which Thou hast given them, they may obtain Thy favour. O Thou Who alone art able to do these things, and things far more exceeding good than these, for us, we praise Thee, through the High Priest and Guardian of our souls, Jesus Christ; through Whom be the glory and the majesty, unto Thee, both now and for all generations, and for ever and ever. Amen.

ANCIENT CHRISTIAN LITURGIES
(perhaps from the fifth century)

30

FROM THE LITURGY OF ST JAMES

We commemorate all faithful and true Christian kings who in the world have founded and established churches and monasteries of God. We also pray for every Christian government, for the clergy and faithful, that they may persevere in virtue. For this let us earnestly beg the Lord. For you are a refuge and salvation, a helping Power and victorious Leader of all who call upon your assistance and have confidence in you. To you belong glory, honour and power with your only Son and the Holy Spirit.

31

FROM THE LITURGY OF ST BASIL

Bless all nations and countries and give us that peace which is from heaven, as well as a peaceful life. Give grace to the kings of this Christian world, the armies and governments that preserve peace. Fill them with your peace, O King of peace, and grant us the favour of your presence. As you have given us everything, take us for yourself. We call upon your holy name and may our lives be imbued with your Holy Spirit and may we not be conquered by the dominion of sin.

32

PART OF THE LITURGY OF
ST JOHN CHRYSOSTOM

We supplicate for our exalted and Christloving King
(and the Royal Family), for his power, victory, continuance, health, salvation and remission of sins, and
that our Lord God especially help him and direct his
way in all things, and subdue under his feet every
enemy and adversary.

33

FROM THE GELASIAN SACRAMENTARY,
EIGHTH CENTURY

O God, in Whose hands are the hearts of Kings,
incline Thy merciful ears to our humble entreaty, and
govern with Thy wisdom our King, Thy servant, that
his counsels may be drawn from Thy fountain and he
may be well pleasing in Thy sight; through Jesus
Christ our Lord. Amen.

34

O God of all Kingdoms, Who art Guardian especially of every Christian realm, grant to Thy servant our King to triumph over every foe, that as he has been consecrated to rule by Thy Divine Providence, so by Thy Protection he may long reign in supremacy and peace; through Jesus Christ our Lord. Amen.

35

FROM THE GREGORIAN SACRAMENTARY, NINTH CENTURY

We beseech Thee, Almighty God, that Thy servant who by Thy mercy hath undertaken the government of the Realm, may also receive the increase of all virtues, and, being beautified therewith, may be able to avoid all sin, and attain to Thee, Who art the Way, the Truth, and the Life, and be acceptable in Thy sight; through Jesus Christ our Lord. Amen.

36

FROM THE MOZARABIC LITURGY, TENTH CENTURY

O heavenly Father, we bend the knee before Thee on behalf of all Kings, Princes, and Governors of this world, beseeching Thee to grant unto them by Thy inspiration, to rule in righteousness, to rejoice in peace, to shine in piety, and to labour for the well-being of the people committed unto them, so that, by the rectitude of the government, all faithful people may live without disturbance in the knowledge of Thee, and labour without hindrance for Thy glory. Amen.

FROM THE *BOOK OF COMMON PRAYER*, 1662

MORNING AND EVENING PRAYER

37

A Prayer for the Queen's Majesty

O Lord our heavenly Father, high and mighty, King of kings, Lord of lords, the only Ruler of princes, who dost from thy throne behold all the dwellers upon earth: Most heartily we beseech thee with thy favour to behold our most gracious Sovereign Lady, Queen Elizabeth; and so replenish her with the grace of thy Holy Spirit, that she may alway incline to thy will, and walk in thy way: Endue her plenteously with heavenly gifts; grant her in health and wealth long to live; strengthen her that she may vanquish and overcome all her enemies, and finally after this life she may attain everlasting joy and felicity; through Jesus Christ our Lord. Amen.

38

A Prayer for the Royal Family

Almighty God, the fountain of all goodness, we humbly beseech thee to bless Elizabeth the Queen Mother, Philip Duke of Edinburgh, Charles Prince of Wales, and all the Royal Family; Endue them with thy Holy Spirit; enrich them with thy heavenly grace; prosper them with all happiness; and bring them to thine everlasting kingdom; through Jesus Christ our Lord. Amen.

THE ORDER FOR HOLY COMMUNION

39

Almighty God, whose kingdom is everlasting, and power infinite: Have mercy upon the whole Church; and so rule the heart of thy chosen servant Elizabeth, our Queen and Governor, that she (knowing whose minister she is) may above all things seek thy honour and glory: and that we and all her subjects (duly considering whose authority she hath) may faithfully serve, honour, and humbly obey her, in thee, and for thee, according to thy blessed Word and ordinance; through Jesus Christ our Lord, who with thee and the Holy Ghost liveth and reigneth, ever one God, world without end. *Amen.*

40

Almighty and everlasting God, we are taught by thy holy Word, that the hearts of Kings are in thy rule and governance, and that thou dost dispose and turn them as it seemeth best to thy godly wisdom: We humbly beseech thee so to dispose and govern the heart of Elizabeth thy servant, our Queen and Governor, that in all her thoughts, words, and works, she may ever seek thy honour and glory, and study to preserve thy people committed to her charge, in wealth, peace and godliness: Grant this, O merciful Father, for thy dear Son's sake, Jesus Christ our Lord. *Amen.*

FROM OTHER OFFICIAL ORDERS OF SERVICE

41

Prayer for the Safety and Preservation of the Queen's Majesty, Set Forth by Authority, 1598

Most gracious God, which by thy word appointedst man to rule thy other creatures, but in wisdom hast lifted up Kings and Princes to command and rule men in their several places: We the people of thy choice, and the subjects of this land, heartily acknowledge thy especial providence in anointing over us so gracious a Princess, so careful of thy glory, so religious in thy fear, so tender of our good, and yet so maligned and shot at by the enemies of thy Gospel, both foreign professed rebels, and homeborn unloyal and discontented runagates, as, were not thy mercy her shield of defence, and thy power the sword of her revenge, long since they had brought her life to the grave, and laid our honour in the dust: Of late especially having prepared and applied very near the sacred body of her royal Majesty a most deadly poison, the purpose strangely did not reveal, and the practice mightily thou did defeat: For which exceeding kindness, most loving Father, we on our knees and from our hearts do give thee thanks, and desire the assistance of thy grace for the amendment of our lives, and the repentance of our sins, which are more deadly than any poison to infect us, and more strong than any foe to overthrow us, and the only motives of thy wrath against us, which if thou canst not but execute upon us, our crying sins so calling for thy vengeance, yet, gracious Lord, enter not so far in just revenge as to quench the light of our land, our most Sovereign Queen, lest the enemies of thy Gospel, her prosperity, and our welfare, take occasion thereby to triumph and say, that thou hast forsaken us; but rather, we humbly beseech thee, prosper her days and prolong her life, and renew her years to the advancement of our peace by Jesus Christ thy only Son, and our only Saviour. To whom, etc.

42

A form of Prayer Necessary to be Used in the Dangerous Times, of War and Pestilence, for the Safety and Preservation of His Majesty and His Realms, 1626

O Lord Creator of all things, and governor of all the Kingdoms of the world, look down, we beseech thee, in mercy upon the estate of this Realm which is now in danger to be assaulted by the enemies thereof. Thou seest, O Lord, how they make a mur-

muring, how they conspire daily and take counsel
together against thee and thine Anointed. We therefore humbly pray thee to extend thine accustomed
goodness to us in the defence of our land, save and
deliver us from the hands of all such as threaten
our destruction. Protect the person of our gracious
Sovereign, direct his Counsels, go forth with the
Armies, be unto him and to us all a wall of brass,
and a strong tower of defence against the face of
our enemies; that so we being safe through thy
mercy, may live to serve thee in thy Church, and
ever give thee praise and glory, through Jesus Christ
our Lord. Amen.

43

A Form of Fasting to be Used Yearly on the Thirtieth of January, Being the Day of the Martyrdom of the Blessed King Charles the First

O most mighty God, terrible in thy judgements, and
wonderful in thy doings toward the children of men;
who in thy heavy displeasure didst suffer the life of
our gracious Sovereign King Charles the First, to
be (as this day) taken away by the hands of cruel
and bloody men: We thy sinful creatures here
assembled before thee, do, on the behalf of all the
people of this land, humbly confess, that they were
the crying sins of this Nation, which brought down

this heavy judgement upon us. But, O gracious God, when thou makest inquisition for blood, lay not the guilt of this innocent blood, (the shedding whereof nothing but the blood of thy Son can expiate), lay it not to the charge of the people of this land; nor let it ever be required of us, or our posterity. Be merciful, O Lord, be merciful unto thy people, whom thou hast redeemed; and be not angry with us for ever: But pardon us for thy mercies' sake, through the merits of thy Son Jesus Christ our Lord. Amen.

44

Blessed Lord, in whose sight the death of thy saints is precious; We magnify thy Name for thine abundant grace bestowed upon our martyred Sovereign; by which he was enabled so cheerfully to follow the steps of his blessed Master and Saviour, in a constant meek suffering of all barbarous indignities, and at last resisting unto blood: and even then, according to the same pattern, praying for his murderers. Let his memory, O Lord, be ever blessed among us; that we may follow the example of his courage and constancy, his meekness and patience, and great charity. And grant, that this our land may be freed from the vengeance of his righteous blood, and thy mercy glorified in the forgiveness of our sins: and all for Jesus

Christ his sake, our only Mediator and Advocate. Amen.

45

A Form of Thanksgiving to be Used Yearly on the Fifth Day of November ('Gunpowder Treason')

Almighty God, who hast in all ages shewed thy Power and Mercy in the miraculous and gracious deliverances of thy Church, and in the protection of righteous and religious Kings and States professing thy holy and eternal truth, from the wicked conspiracies, and malicious practices of all the enemies thereof: We yield thee our unfeigned thanks and praise, for the wonderful and mighty Deliverance of our gracious Sovereign King James the First, the Queen, the Prince, and all the Royal Branches, with the Nobility, Clergy, and Commons of England, then assembled in Parliament, by Popish treachery appointed as sheep to the slaughter, in a most barbarous and savage manner, beyond the examples of former ages. From this unnatural Conspiracy, not our merit, but thy mercy; not our foresight, but thy providence delivered us: And therefore not unto us, O Lord, not unto us, but unto thy Name be ascribed all honour and glory, in all Churches of the saints, from generation to generation; through Jesus Christ our Lord. Amen.

46

A Prayer Added After the Landing of the Prince of Orange

Almighty God and heavenly Father, who of thy gracious Providence, and tender mercy towards us, didst prevent the malice and imaginations of our enemies, by discovering and confounding their horrible and wicked Enterprize, plotted and intended this day to have been executed against the King, and the whole State of England, for the subversion of the Government and Religion established among us; and didst likewise upon this day wonderfully conduct thy Servant King William, and bring him safely into England, to preserve us from the attempts of our enemies to bereave us of our Religion and Laws: we most humbly praise and magnify thy most glorious Name for thy unspeakable goodness towards us, expressed in both these acts of thy mercy. We confess it has been of thy mercy alone, that we are not consumed: For our sins have cried to heaven against us; and our iniquities justly called for vengeance upon us. But thou hast not dealt with us after our sins, not rewarded us after our iniquities; nor given us over, as we deserved, to be a prey to our enemies; but hast in mercy delivered us from their malice, and preserved us from death and destruction. Let the consideration of this thy repeated goodness, O Lord, work in us true repentance, that iniquity may not be our ruin. And increase in us more and more a lively faith and love, fruitful in all holy obedience; that thou mayest still continue thy favour, with the light of thy Gospel, to us and our posterity for evermore; and that for thy dear Son's sake, Jesus Christ our only Mediator and Advocate. Amen.

47

A Form of Prayer with Thanksgiving to Almighty God for Having Put an End to the Great Rebellion by the Restitution of the King and Royal Family, and the Restoration of the Government After Many Years' Interruption

O Lord God of our salvation, who has been exceedingly gracious unto this land, and by thy miraculous providence didst deliver us out of our miserable confusions; by restoring to us, and to his own just and undoubted Rights, our then most gracious Sovereign Lord, King Charles the Second, notwithstanding all the power and malice of his enemies; and, by placing him on the Throne of these Kingdoms, didst restore also unto us the publick and free profession of thy true Religion and Worship, together with our former Peace and Prosperity, to the great comfort and joy of our hearts: We are here now before thee, with all due thankfulness to acknowledge thine unspeakable goodness herein, as upon the Day shewed unto us, and to offer unto thee our sacrifice of praise for the same; humbly beseeching thee to accept this our unfeigned, though unworthy oblation of ourselves; vowing all holy obedience in thought, word and work, unto thy Divine Majesty: and promising all loyal and dutiful Allegiance to thine Anointed Servant now set over us, and to his Heirs after him; whom we beseech thee to bless with all increase of grace, honour and happiness, in this world, and to crown him with immortality and glory in the world to come, for Jesus Christ his sake our only Lord and Saviour. Amen.

48

Thanksgiving for the Recovery of His Royal Highness the Prince of Wales, 1872

O Father of mercies and God of all comfort, we thank thee that thou hast heard the prayers of this nation in the day of our trial: We praise and magnify thy glorious name for that thou hast raised thy Servant Albert Edward Prince of Wales from the bed of sickness: Thou castest down and thou liftest up, and health and strength are thy gifts: We pray thee to perfect the recovery of thy Servant, and to crown him day by day with more abundant blessings both for body and soul; through Jesus Christ our Lord. Amen.

THE ACCESSION SERVICE
(On the Anniversary of the Day of Accession of the Reigning Sovereign)

49

1576 (QUEEN ELIZABETH I)

O Lord God, most merciful Father, who as upon this day, placing thy servant our Sovereign and gracious Queen Elizabeth in the kingdom, didst deliver thy people of England from danger of war and oppression, both of bodies by tyranny, and of conscience by superstition, restoring peace and true religion, with liberty both of bodies and minds, and hast continued the same thy blessings, without all desert on our part, now by the space of these *eighteen* years: we who are in memory of these thy great benefits assembled here together, most humbly beseech thy fatherly goodness to grant us grace, that we may in word, deed, and heart, shew ourselves thankful and obedient unto thee for the same: and that our Queen through thy grace may in all honour, goodness, and godliness, long and many years reign over us, and we obey and enjoy her, with the continuance of thy great blessings, which thou hast by her thy minister poured upon us: This we beseech thee to grant unto us, for thy dear Son Jesus Christ's sake, our Lord and Saviour. Amen.

50

1625 (KING CHARLES I)

O Lord, thou hast dealt graciously with our land: and we thy unworthy creatures acknowledge ourselves infinitely blessed in thy servant our dread Sovereign King Charles, whom thou hast chosen and anointed to rule over us: and we are at this time here gathered together before heaven and before thee, to make grateful commemoration of the time, and of the day wherein this thine unspeakable goodness began to be poured upon us, and to offer up our vows and sacrifices of thanksgiving, and praise unto thy glorious Name, which cannot worthily of us be praised: humbly beseeching thee to accept the unworthy oblation of ourselves, vowing all obedience in thought, word and work unto thy divine Majesty, and promising in thee, and for thee unto this our King all loyal and faithful allegiance, and to his seed, his heirs and successors after him in all generations, whom we beseech thee to follow with all increasing honour and happiness in this world, and to crown with immortality, and glory in the world to come, for Jesus Christ his sake our only Lord and Saviour. Amen.

51

1704 (QUEEN ANNE)

Blessed Lord, Who hast called Christian Princes to the defence of Thy faith, and hast made it their duty to promote the spiritual welfare, together with the temporal interest of their people; we acknowledge with humble and thankful hearts Thy great goodness to us, in setting Thy Servant, our most gracious Queen, over this Church and Nation; give her, we beseech Thee, all those heavenly graces that are requisite for so high a trust. Let the work of Thee her God prosper in her hands; let her eyes behold the success of her designs for the service of Thy true Religion established amongst us, and make her a blessed instrument of protecting and advancing Thy Truth, whenever it is persecuted and oppressed; let hypocrisy and profaneness, superstitions and idolatry, fly before her face; let not heresies and false doctrines disturb the peace of the Church, nor schisms and causeless divisions weaken it; but grant us to be of one heart and one mind in serving Thee our God, and obeying her according to Thy will. And that these blessings may be continued to after-ages, let there never be one wanting in her house to succeed her in the government of this United Kingdom, that our posterity may see her children's children, and peace upon Israel; so we that are Thy people, and sheep of Thy pasture, shall give Thee thanks for ever, and will always be showing forth Thy praise

from generation to generation; through Jesus Christ
Thy Son our Lord. Amen.

52

1837 (QUEEN VICTORIA)

Most gracious God, who hast set thy servant Victoria
our Queen upon the Throne of her Ancestors, we
most humbly beseech thee to protect her on the same
from all the dangers to which she may be exposed;
Hide her from the gathering together of the froward,
and from the insurrection of wicked doers; Do thou
weaken the hands, blast the designs, and defeat the
enterprises of all her enemies, that no secret conspiracies, nor open violences, may disquiet her
Reign; but that, being safely kept under the shadow
of thy wing, and supported by thy power, she may
triumph over all opposition; that so the world may
acknowledge thee to be her defender and mighty
deliverer in all difficulties and adversities; through
Jesus Christ our Lord. Amen.

53

1953 (QUEEN ELIZABETH II)

O God, who providest for thy people by thy power, and rulest over them in love: Vouchsafe so to bless thy Servant our Queen, that under her this nation may be wisely governed, and thy Church may serve thee in all godly quietness; and grant that she being devoted to thee with her whole heart, and persevering in good works unto the end, may, by thy guidance, come to thine everlasting kingdom; through Jesus Christ thy Son our Lord, who liveth and reigneth with thee and the Holy Ghost, ever one God, world without end. Amen.

54

O Lord our God, who upholdest and governest all things by the word of thy power: receive our humble prayers for our Sovereign Lady Elizabeth, set over us by thy grace and providence to be our Queen; and together with her, bless, we beseech thee, our gracious Elizabeth, the Queen Mother, Philip, Duke of Edinburgh, Charles, Prince of Wales, and all the Royal Family; that they, ever trusting in thy goodness, protected by thy power, and crowned with thy gracious and endless favour, may long continue before thee in peace and safety, joy and honour, and after death may obtain everlasting life and glory; by the merits and mediation of Christ Jesus our Saviour, who with thee and the Holy Ghost liveth and reigneth, ever one God, world without end.

55

Almighty God, who rulest over all the kingdoms of the world, and dost order them according to thy good pleasure: We yield thee unfeigned thanks, for that thou wast pleased, *as on this day*, to set thy Servant our Sovereign Lady, Queen Elizabeth, upon the Throne of this Realm. Let thy wisdom be her guide, and let thine arm strengthen her; let truth and justice, holiness and righteousness, peace and charity, abound in her days; direct all her counsels and endeavours to thy glory, and the welfare of her subjects; give us grace to obey her cheerfully for conscience sake, and let her always possess the hearts of her people; let her reign be long and prosperous, and crown her with everlasting life in the world to come; through Jesus Christ our Lord. Amen.

THE 1928 PRAYER BOOK

56

Almighty God, the fountain of all goodness, we humbly beseech thee to bless our Sovereign Lord, King George, the Parliaments in all his dominions, and all who are set in authority under him; that they may order all things in wisdom, righteousness and peace, to the honour of thy holy name, and the good of thy Church and people; through Jesus Christ our Lord. Amen.

THE ALTERNATIVE SERVICE BOOK 1980

57

Almighty God, the fountain of all goodness, bless our Sovereign Lady, Queen Elizabeth, and all who are in authority under her; that they may order all things in wisdom and equity, righteousness and peace, to the honour of your name, and the good of your Church and people; through Jesus Christ our Lord. Amen.

58

Almighty God, the fountain of all goodness, bless, we pray, Elizabeth the Queen Mother, Philip Duke of Edinburgh, Prince Charles of Wales, and all the Royal Family. Endue them with your Holy Spirit; enrich them with your heavenly grace; prosper them with all happiness; and bring them to your everlasting kingdom; through Jesus Christ our Lord. Amen.

ANNIVERSARIES AND COMMEMORATIONS

59

QUEEN VICTORIA'S GOLDEN JUBILEE (1887)

Almighty God, we humbly offer unto Thy Divine Majesty our prayers and hearty thanksgivings for our gracious Sovereign Lady Queen Victoria, unto whom Thou hast accomplished full fifty years of Sovereignty.

We praise Thee that through Thy grace She hath kept the charge Thou gavest Her in the day when

Thou didst set the Crown upon Her head, bidding Her 'to do Justice, stay the growth of iniquity, and protect the Holy Church of God; to help and defend widows and orphans; to restore the things gone to decay, maintain the things that are restored: punish and reform what is amiss, and confirm what is in good order; to keep the Royal Law and Lively Oracles of God.'

We bless Thee that Thou hast heard, through sorrow and through joy, our prayer that She should always possess the hearts of Her people. And we humbly pray Thee that for the years to come She may rejoice in Thy strength, and at the Resurrection of the Just enter into Thine immortal kingdom; through Jesus Christ our Lord. Amen.

60

QUEEN VICTORIA'S DIAMOND
JUBILEE (1897)

O God, which providest for Thy people by Thy power, and rulest over them in love, grant unto Thy servant our Queen the spirit of wisdom and government, that being devoted unto Thee with all her heart, she may so wisely govern this kingdom, that in her time the Church may be in safety and Christian devotion may continue in peace; that so, persevering in good works unto the end, she may by Thy guidance come to Thine everlasting Kingdom, through Jesus Christ Thy Son our Lord, who liveth and reigneth with Thee and the Holy Ghost ever one God, world without end. Amen.

61

QUEEN VICTORIA'S MEMORIAL SERVICE (1901)

O God, whose Providence ruleth all things both in heaven and earth, by whom kings reign and princes decree justice, we thank thee for all the blessings which thou hast bestowed upon us through our Queen Victoria lately taken from us. We thank thee for the wisdom of her counsels, for the care and love with which she watched over her people, for the bright example of her noble life, for the prosperity which we enjoyed during her happy reign; and we pray thee to fill our hearts with gratitude for all these benefits, and to give us grace that we may use the memory of them as a perpetual call to live according to thy will, for the good of our fellow men and the glory of thy great Name, through Jesus Christ our Lord. Amen.

62

KING EDWARD VII'S
MEMORIAL SERVICE (1910)

O Lord our Heavenly Father, Almighty and Ever-lasting God, by whom kings reign and princes decree justice: We remember before thee our late Sovereign Lord, King Edward, in thankfulness for the blessings which thou hast bestowed upon us through his reign; for the wisdom of his rule, and the faithfulness with which he served the people committed to his charge; for his continual effort to further and maintain peace among all nations; and for his watchful care of the sick and of the poor. And we beseech thee to give us grace that, having these thy mercies in remembrance, we may with one heart and one mind set forward the welfare of this Land and Empire, and hasten the coming of thy kingdom of peace and goodwill among men; through Jesus Christ our Lord. Amen.

63

KING GEORGE V'S
MEMORIAL SERVICE (1936)

O Lord our Heavenly Father, Almighty and Everlasting God, by whom kings reign and princes decree justice: We remember before thee our late Sovereign Lord, King George, in thankfulness for the blessings which thou hast bestowed upon us through his reign; for the example he set of unwearied devotion to duty; for his steadfast courage in years of war and manifold anxieties; and for the love and loyalty borne to him by a great family of peoples in all parts of the world. And we beseech thee to give us grace that, having these thy mercies in remembrance, we may with one heart and one mind set forward the welfare of this Land and Empire, and hasten the coming of thy kingdom of peace and goodwill among men; through Jesus Christ our Lord. Amen.

PRAYERS BY ANGLICAN DIVINES

64

JOHN HAMILTON (1511-71), ARCHBISHOP OF ST ANDREWS

Bless, O Lord, those whom Thou hast set over us both in Church and State; govern their hearts in Thy fear, and guide their understandings to do those things which will be acceptable to Thee, and beneficial to Thy Church and this Kingdom. Give the King loving and loyal subjects, and confound and defeat his open and secret enemies. Comfort the comfortless and helpless; show the light of Thy Truth to those who wander out of the right way; give to all sinners true repentance; strengthen and assist with Thy grace those who have begun well, that they may persevere in goodness. To all our friends, kindred, and enemies, give all Thy good blessings. Keep us from all evil, and make us to continue in Thy service to our lives' end; and after the course of this life is ended, bring us to Thine everlasting Kingdom; through Jesus Christ our Lord. Amen.

65

LANCELOT ANDREWES (1555–1626), BISHOP OF WINCHESTER

King of kings and Lord of lords,
    Remember all rulers
whom thou has appointed to bear rule
    on the earth.
And among the first, be mindful of
    our gracious Queen,
And prosper her in all things;
And put into her heart good designs
    for thy church.
And for all thy people committed
    to her charge.
Grant unto her profound and undisturbed peace
    that in the tranquillity of her reign
we may lead a quiet and peaceful life,
    in all godliness and honesty.

66

WILLIAM LAUD (1573–1645), ARCHBISHOP OF CANTERBURY

O Lord our God, Who hast ever been a gracious
Helper and Friend to our country, our Refuge and
Strength from one generation to another, we beseech

Thee of Thy mercy to bless our Sovereign Lord, King James, with Thy heavenly grace, that in all his many and great anxieties for the peace and welfare of his Realm, he may find rest and strength in Thee, and be alway consoled by the loyalty and love of his people. We pray that it may please Thee to spare him to us for many years yet to come, and to make us worthy of so great a privilege by faithful allegiance to his person and his throne, by following him in the steps of his and our Divine Master, even Jesus Christ our Lord. Amen.

67

O Lord, grant the King a long life, that his years may be rich with Thy blessing; furnish him with wise and sage counsels, and give him a heart of courage and constancy to pursue them. O prepare Thy loving mercy and faithfulness for him, that they may preserve him; so will we always sing praises unto Thy Name; through Jesus Christ our Lord. Amen.

68

JOHN COSIN (1594–1672), BISHOP OF DURHAM

For the King

O Almightie and everlasting God, Creator and Lord of all things, give eare we beseech thee, unto our humble prayers, and multiply thy blessings upon thy Servant, our Soveraigne King Charles, whom in all lowly devotion we commend unto thy high Majestie: that Hee being strengthened with the faith of Abraham, endued with the mildnes of Moses, armed with the magnanimitie of Joshua, exalted with the humilitie of David, beautified with the wisedome of Salomon, and replenished with the goodnes and holinesse of them all, He may walke uprightly before thee, in the way of righteousnesse, and like a mightie King, may be powerfull over his enemies, governing his people with equitie, and preserving thy Church with Truth and Peace, through Jesus Christ our Lord. Amen.

69

For the Queen

Almightie God, the Fountaine of all mercy, we humbly beseech thee to powre downe the Riches of thine abundant goodnesse upon the Head of thine Handmaid, our most gracious Q. Marie, that shee being continually beautified with the Royall ornaments of thy heavenly Grace, may be holy and devout as Hester, loving to the King as Rachel, fruitfull as Leah, wise as Rebecca, faithfull and obedient as Sarah: and with long life and glory continuing in her High & Princely estate here, shee may at last be brought to the great happinesse of thine everlasting estate hereafter, through Jesus Christ our Lord. Amen.

70

JEREMY TAYLOR (1613–67)
BISHOP OF DOWN AND CONNOR

Eternal God, who rulest in the kingdoms of men: Grant, we most humbly beseech thee, honour and safety to our sovereign; peace throughout the commonwealth of his peoples; promotion to true religion; encouragement to learning and godly living; a patient service to the concord of the world; and, by all these, glory to thy holy name; for his sake to whom thou hast given all power in heaven and earth, even our Lord and Saviour Jesus Christ.

71

We pray unto Thee, O great King of heaven and earth, for all Christian Kings, Princes, Governors, and States. Crown them with justice and peace, and with the love of God, and the love of their people. Let holiness unto the Lord be on their foreheads, invest them with the armour of righteousness, and let the anointing from above make them sacred and venerable, wise and holy; that, being servants of the King of kings, friends of religion, ministers of justice, patrons of the poor, they may at last inherit a portion in the Kingdom of our Lord and Saviour Jesus Christ. Grant this for the sake of Christ Jesus, Who is the King of kings and Lord of lords. Amen.

72

O God of infinite mercy, remember all Sovereign Rulers; preserve their persons in health and honour, their crowns in wealth and dignity, their kingdoms in peace and plenty, the churches under their protection in piety and knowledge, and a strict and holy religion. Keep them perpetually in Thy fear and favour, and crown them with glory and immortality; through Jesus Christ our Lord. Amen.

NINETEENTH- AND EARLY TWENTIETH-CENTURY PRAYERS

73

DR THOMAS ARNOLD (1795–1842)

O Lord, Who by Thy holy Apostles hast commanded us to make prayers and intercessions for all men, we implore Thy blessing more especially upon this our country, upon its Government and upon its people. May Thy Holy Spirit be with our rulers, with the King, and all who are in authority under him. Grant that they may govern in Thy faith and fear, striving to put down all evil, and to encourage and support all that is good. Give Thy Spirit of wisdom to those whose business it is to make laws for us. Grant that they may understand and feel, how great a work Thou hast given them to do, that they may not do it lightly or foolishly, or from any evil passion, or in ignorance; but gravely, soberly, and with a godly spirit, enacting always things just, and things wise, and things merciful, to the putting away of all wrong and oppression, and to the advancement of the true welfare of Thy people. Give peace in our time, O Lord. Preserve both us and our Government from the evil spirit of ambition and pride, and teach us to value and to labour with all sincerity, to preserve peace at home and peace with all nations, showing forth a spirit of meekness, as becomes those who call themselves

Christ's servants. Save us from all those national sins which expose us most justly to Thy heavy judgments. From unbelief and profaneness, from injustice and oppression, from a careless and worldly spirit, working and enjoying, with no thought of Thee; from these, and all other sins, be pleased to preserve us, and give us each one for himself a holy watchfulness, that we may not by our sins add to the guilt and punishment of our country, but may strive to keep ourselves pure and holy, and to bring down Thy blessing upon ourselves, and all who belong to us. These things and all else which may be good for our temporal, and for our spiritual welfare, we humbly beseech Thee to grant, in the name and for the sake of Thy dear Son, Jesus Christ our Lord. Amen.

74

DR JAMES MARTINEAU (1805–1900)

Almighty Lord, of Whose righteous Will all things are, and were created; Thou hast gathered our people into a great nation, and sent them to sow beside all waters, and multiply sure dwellings on the earth. Deepen the root of our life in everlasting righteousness. Make us equal to our high trusts, reverent in the use of freedom, just in the exercise of power, generous in the protection of weakness. With all Thy blessings, bless Thy servant William our King, with

all the members of the Royal House. Fill his heart
and theirs with such loyalty to Thee, that his people
may be exalted by their loyalty to him. To our legislators and counsellors give insight and faithfulness,
that our laws may clearly speak the right, and our
judges purely interpret them. May wisdom and knowledge be the stability of our times, and our deepest
trust be in Thee, the Lord of Nations, and the King
of Kings, even Jesus Christ our Lord. Amen.

75

THE REVD W.E. SCUDAMORE (1813–81)

Bless, O Lord, we beseech thee, our Queen and
parliament, our judges and magistrates, and all who
bear any office or rule in the state. Save us from the
sins that most easily beset us; bless every effort for
the well-being of our people; and make us a nation
fearing thee and doing righteousness, to the glory of
thy holy name; through Jesus Christ our Lord.

76

THE REVD ROBERT COLLYER (1823–1912)

O Almighty and Everlasting God, we pray Thee to bless and preserve Thy Servant, King Edward who in Thy good Providence rules these realms. Grant to him and all his councillors, that out of godly hearts they may devise godly measures. May they seek first Thy kingdom and righteousness. May they yield obedience to our King and rulers as Thy appointed ministers. Thus may our lives be quiet and peaceable in all godliness and honesty. Thou Who hearest prayer, hear us, for the sake of Him Thou hearest always, Jesus Christ our Lord. Amen.

77

THE REVD FR R.M. BENSON SSJE (1824–1915)

Almighty God, the Source of all rightful power amongst us Thy creatures, give Thy grace unto our Sovereign Lord King George and all the Royal Family, that, acknowledging their power to be dependent on Thy supreme Majesty, they may come to reign with Thee in Thine everlasting Kingdom. Grant also that the spirit of godliness ruling their hearts, may quicken all those who are round about them to a sense of the nothingness of earthly glory, and the necessity of striving after that which is eternal: so may all their counsels and actions be directed to Thine honour, and the nation at large be brought to participate in Thine acceptance of their faith; through Jesus Christ our Lord. Amen.

78

THE REVD L.R. TULLIETT (1825–97)

O Father of all, we humbly beseech Thee to show Thy mercy to the whole world. Let the Gospel of Thy Son run and be glorified throughout the earth. Let it be known by those who as yet know it not, let it be obeyed by all who profess and call themselves Christians. Continue Thy loving kindness, O Lord, to this Nation to which we belong, and increase in us true religion. Multiply Thy blessings upon our Queen, and all the Royal Family, giving them grace in all things to set forward Thy glory and the public good. Endue with Thy best gifts all who minister, that they may earnestly feed Thy flock. Visit in compassion all the children of affliction, relieve their necessities, and lighten their burdens, giving them patience and submission to Thy holy will, and in due time deliver them from all their troubles. Into Thy hand we commend all Thy people everywhere. Hear us, O Lord, we humbly beseech Thee, for the sake of Christ Jesus our Lord. Amen.

79

THE RT REVD H.C.G. MOULE,
BISHOP OF DURHAM (1841–1920)

O Thou Who art the Prince of the Kings and peoples
of the earth, receive our prayer, we beseech Thee,
for our own Country. We pray Thee for our King,
for the Royal Family; for all the Ministers of State,
and all Members of Parliament; that Thy power and
mercy may rule those who guide, and order those
who legislate. If it please Thee, bring all their wills
into true accord with Thy will. Let all seek the good
not of parties, but of the whole people. Let them
govern in the fear of God, and not in too much fear
of man, or for any private advantage of their own.
O Lord, we deserve chastisement at Thy hands and
not prosperity. To us belongeth confusion of face,
because we have sinned against Thee; yet for Thy
Name's sake bless us, cleanse us, and defend us, and
make use of us in the world for Thee; to the praise
and honour of Jesus Christ our Lord. Amen.

80

Let Thy mercy and blessing, O Lord of Lords, rest
upon our land and nation; upon all the powers which
Thou hast ordained over us; our King, and all in
authority under him; the Ministers of State, the great

Councils of the Nation; all Judges and Magistrates; that we may lead a quiet and peaceable life in all godliness and honesty. Rule the hearts of men in all classes of our people; and in these days of restlessness and self-will, draw all together in true brotherhood and sympathy. Rebuke the power of unbelief and of superstition, and preserve to us Thy pure Word in its liberty and glory even to the end of days; through Jesus Christ our Lord. Amen.

81

THE EARL OF MEATH (1841–1909)

O God, Who hast made us members of the British Empire, and hast bound us together by one King and one Flag, may we ever live in remembrance of our great responsibilities, and be mindful that 'righteousness exalteth a nation'. Help us to seek to excel in the practice of faith, courage, duty, self-discipline, fair dealing, even justice, and true sympathy, that, as loyal patriots and good citizens, we may each individually aid in elevating the British character, and as a God-fearing and a God-loving people glorify Thee, the King of kings and Lord of lords; through Jesus Christ Thy Son. Amen.

82

THE REVD H. STOBART

Remember, O Lord, according to the multitude of Thy mercies, all those whom Thou hast appointed to rule over the several nations of the earth, especially Thy servant, our King; and grant to Thy Church faithful and wise pastors, who may enlighten it, both by their life and doctrine, and having turned many to righteousness, may shine in glory, as stars, for ever and ever; through Jesus Christ our Lord. Amen.

83

O God, the God of the spirits of all flesh, we humbly beseech Thee to accept our intercessions on behalf of all men. We pray for Thy universal Church, that it may be guided by Thy Holy Spirit in the way of truth and peace. O Lord, save our King. Bless Thy servants the clergy and ministers, and grant that they may shine as lights in the world, and adorn the doctrine of God our Saviour in all things. We commend, O Lord, to Thy Fatherly goodness, our relations, friends, and neighbours, and all who desire, or ought to be specially remembered in our prayers. Succour the poor and needy, bind up the broken-hearted, have mercy on the sick and dying, and help us, by Thy

Grace, to live nearer to Thee day by day; through Jesus Christ our Lord. Amen.

84

THE REVD W. BELLARS

Bless, we beseech Thee, merciful Lord, our Country, and all its colonies and dependencies. Give Thine abundant grace to our King, and to all who bear office throughout the realm, that in all things we may be governed righteously and in Thy fear, and grant to us, not only such outward prosperity as is according to Thy will, but, above all things, such virtue and true religion that Thy Holy Name may be ever glorified in the midst of us; through Jesus Christ our Lord. Amen.

85

ANON., *A TREASURY OF DEVOTION*, 1869

O Lord, Who of Thy favour towards us hast set George our King, to reign over us, keep him, we beseech Thee, under Thy almighty protection, save and defend him from all his enemies, both ghostly and bodily; give him grace to rule Thy people according to Thy will, that he may here govern to Thy honour and glory, and after this life receive and enjoy the inheritance of Thy heavenly kingdom, in the life and bliss that never shall have an end; through Jesus Christ our Lord. Amen.

86

LADY MARGARET HALL, 1902

O Almighty God, Who rulest over all the earth, and guidest the affairs of men, we humbly beseech Thee to govern and bless all connected with our land and nation. We pray for our King, Queen, and all the members of the Royal Family. We pray for the Prime Minister, the Cabinet, and Ministers of State, that Thy wisdom may be their guide in foreign and domestic policy, for the maintenance of high principle, and the advancement of justice, truth, holiness, peace, and love. We pray for the Legislature, both the Lords and Commons, that Thou wilt direct and prosper their deliberations to the advancement of Thy glory and the welfare of the realm, giving them freedom from party spirit and a hearty desire for the good of their country. We pray especially for all Christian members of Parliament that they may not be ashamed to confess the faith of Christ crucified, but may speak out and vote manfully on the side of righteousness. We also pray for the Bishops in the

House of Lords, that they may show themselves in all things an example of good works to others; and finally we pray that all righteous reforms may be pressed forward and passed by Parliament, and that all Thy Christian people may learn to pray more earnestly for Thy guidance in all political matters, and that all things may be done with a single eye to Thy glory, through Jesus Christ our Lord. Amen.

87

'J.E.W.', 1914

Thou Wonderful, Counsellor, King of kings and Lord of lords, send Thy blessing on our Royal Sovereign in his care. Strong in counsel, patient in action, pure in motive, striving for the welfare of his people, may his great kingdom ever be Thy kingdom, Thy law his law, Thy glory his renown. And for us who are his subjects grant us so to walk worthy of his royal command that our humble service may never be his shame; through Jesus Christ our Lord. Amen.

88

FROM THE *DIVINE OFFICE OF THE CATHOLIC APOSTOLIC CHURCH*, 1925

We pray for all estates of men in Christian lands; for kings, princes, and governors; for judges and magistrates; for nobles and men of estate; and for all the people. We beseech Thee to put Thine honour and majesty on all who are in authority, and so to dispose and order the affairs of all nations, that righteousness and truth may prevail; that injustice, cruelty, and fraud may be defeated; and that we may lead quiet and peaceable lives, in all godliness and honesty. Especially in this land, we remember before Thee our gracious Sovereign King George, our gracious Queen Mary, Alexandra the Queen Mother, Edward Prince of Wales, and all the Royal Family. Give wisdom and understanding, we beseech Thee, [to the High Court of Parliament and] to all ministers of state and officers of government; and let Thy blessing rest on all our fellow-subjects in this United Kingdom, and in all the colonies and dependencies of the realm.

ROMAN CATHOLIC PRAYERS IN ENGLAND AND WALES

89

Prayer for the Queen formerly sung after the principal Mass (especially a sung Mass) on Sundays in England and Wales: It is based on the collect in the Mass *Pro Rege* in the *Missale Romanum* (1570).

Domine, salvam fac reginam nostram Elizabeth, et exaudi nos in die qua invocaverimus te.

Oremus.

Quaesumus, omnipotens Deus: ut famula tua Elizabeth, regina nostra, qui tua miseratione suscepit regni gubernacula, virtutum etiam omnium percipiat incrementa; quibus decenter ornata, et vitiorum monstra devitare, [hostes superare,] et ad te, qui via, veritas et vita es, cum principe consorte et prole regia gratiosa valeat pervenire. Per Christum Dominum nostrum. Amen.

90

ENGLISH VERSION (1953)

For the Queen

Versicle   O Lord, save Elizabeth, our Queen.
Response   And hear us in the day when we shall call
             upon thee.

Almighty God, we pray for thy servant Elizabeth, now by thy mercy reigning over us. Adorn her yet more with every virtue, remove all evil from her path (and vanquish her enemies); that with her consort and all the royal family she may come at last in grace to thee, who art the way, the truth, and the life. Through Christ our Lord. Amen.

91

There was an older prayer sometimes used after Mass: It dates from 1886.

For Our Temporal Sovereign

Versicle   O Lord, save the king.
Response   And hear us in the day that we shall call
             upon Thee.

Let us pray.

O God, by whom kings reign, and the princes of the earth exercise their power; O God, who art the strength and support of those kingdoms that serve Thee; mercifully hear our prayers, and defend Thy servant N. our [king *or* queen] from all dangers; and grant that [his *or* her] safety may conduce to the peace and welfare of Thy people. Through Christ our Lord. Amen.

92

The present-day provision is as follows:

MISSALE ROMANUM (1970)

Pro Supremo Nationis Moderatore

Deus, cui potestates humanae deserviunt,
da famulo tuo (regi nostro) N.
prosperum suae dignitatis effectum,
in qua, te semper timens tibique placere contendens,
populo sibi credito liberam ordinis tranquillitatem
iugiter procuret et servet.
Per Dominum.

93

Translation of the above:

THE ROMAN MISSAL (1974)

For the King or Head of State

God our Father,
all earthly powers must serve you.
Help your servant N. [our King N.]
to fulfil his responsibilities worthily and well.
By honouring and striving to please you at all
   times,
may he secure peace and freedom
for the people entrusted to him.
We ask this through our Lord Jesus Christ.

PRAYERS FROM THE CORONATION SERVICE (1953)

94

OPENING COLLECT

O God, who providest for thy people by thy power, and rulest over them in love: Grant unto this thy servant Elizabeth, our Queen, the Spirit of wisdom and government, that being devoted unto thee with her whole heart, she may so wisely govern, that in her time thy Church may be in safety, and Christian devotion may continue in peace; that so persevering in good works unto the end, she may by thy mercy come to thine everlasting kingdom; through Jesus Christ, thy Son, our Lord, who liveth and reigneth with thee in the unity of the Holy Ghost, one God for ever and ever. Amen.

95

AT THE BLESSING OF THE OIL

O Lord and heavenly Father, the exalter of the humble and the strength of thy chosen, who by anointing with Oil didst of old make and consecrate kings, priests, and prophets, to teach and govern thy people Israel: Bless and sanctify thy chosen servant Elizabeth, who by our office and ministry is now to be anointed with this Oil and consecrated Queen: Strengthen her, O Lord, with the Holy Ghost the Comforter; Confirm and stablish her with thy free and princely Spirit, the Spirit of wisdom and government, the Spirit of counsel and ghostly strength, the Spirit of knowledge and true godliness, and fill her, O Lord, with the Spirit of thy holy fear, now and for ever; through Jesus Christ our Lord. Amen.

96

AT THE ANOINTING

Our Lord Jesus Christ, the Son of God, who by his Father was anointed with the Oil of gladness above his fellows, by his holy Anointing pour down upon your Head and Heart the blessing of the Holy Ghost, and prosper the works of your Hands: that by the assistance of his heavenly grace you may govern and preserve the Peoples committed to your charge in wealth, peace, and godliness; and after a long and glorious course of ruling a temporal kingdom wisely, justly, and religiously, you may at last be made partaker of an eternal kingdom, through the same Jesus Christ our Lord. Amen.

97

AT THE PRESENTATION OF THE
SWORD OF STATE

Hear our prayers, O Lord, we beseech thee, and so direct and support thy servant Queen Elizabeth, that she may not bear the Sword in vain; but may use it as the minister of God for the terror and punishment of evildoers, and for the protection and encouragement of those that do well, through Jesus Christ our Lord. Amen.

98

AT THE CROWNING

O God the Crown of the faithful: Bless we beseech thee this Crown, and so sanctify thy servant Elizabeth upon whose head this day thou dost place it for a sign of royal majesty, that she may be filled by thine abundant grace with all princely virtues: through the King eternal Jesus Christ our Lord. Amen.

99

THE BENEDICTION

The Lord bless you and keep you. The Lord protect you in all your ways and prosper all your handywork. Amen.

The Lord give you faithful Parliaments and quiet Realms; sure defence against all enemies; fruitful lands and a prosperous industry; wise counsellors and upright magistrates; leaders of integrity in learning and labour; a devout, learned and useful clergy; honest, peaceable and dutiful citizens. Amen.

May Wisdom and Knowledge be the Stability of your Times, and the Fear of the Lord your Treasure. Amen.

The Lord who hath made you Queen over these Peoples give you increase of grace, honour and happiness in this world, and make you partaker of his eternal felicity in the world to come. Amen.

FROM THE SILVER JUBILEE PRAYERS (1977)

100

Almighty God, who rulest over the kingdoms of the world, and dost order them according to thy good pleasure: we yield thee unfeigned thanks for that thou wast pleased in the year of our Lord one thousand nine hundred and fifty-two, to set thy servant our Sovereign Lady, Queen Elizabeth, upon the throne of this realm. Let thy wisdom be her guide and let thine arm strengthen her; let truth and justice, holiness and righteousness, peace and charity, abound in her days. Direct all her counsels and endeavours to thy glory and the welfare of her subjects; give us grace to obey her cheerfully for conscience sake, and let her always possess the hearts of her people; let her reign be long and prosperous, and crown her with everlasting life in the world to come; through Jesus Christ Our Lord. Amen.

101

Almighty God, our heavenly Father,
bless Elizabeth our Queen,
whose jubilee we now celebrate.
Help her to fulfil her responsibilities;
that by her influence

she may maintain unity, goodwill and peace
   among her peoples
and finally attain to the eternal kingdom of Christ;
who is alive and reigns
with you and the Holy Spirit,
one God now and for ever. Amen.

102

Minister Let us pray.

Heavenly Father, we give you thanks for
   the wonder of creation,
for the gift of human life and for the
   blessing of human fellowship;
for Christ, your living Word,
through whom we are taught
   the perfect way of life and the royalty of
   service;
and for your Spirit, who offers his gifts to
   us for the common good.

All   **We thank you, Lord.**

Minister For the blessing of community in our
      Nation and Commonwealth,
      and for those who have used your gifts
      to strengthen and enrich its life.

All   **We thank you, Lord**.

Minister Today especially we give you thanks for
          our Sovereign Lady, Queen Elizabeth,
          and for her family;
        for her long and tireless service to our
          world-wide family of nations;
        for her profession of faith in you by word
          and deed;
        for her example of unselfish devotion
          and duty;
        for her care for her people, and her
          concern for them
          at all times and in all places.

All   **We thank you, Lord**.

Minister Continue in her and her family, we pray,
          your royal gifts of service;
        the vision of your will for her people;
        wisdom to fulfil her vocation of leadership
          in a Commonwealth of many races;
        strength and courage to carry out the
          duties of her calling;
        and grant her always the assurance of
          your presence, your power, and your love.
        Lord, in your mercy

All   **Hear our prayer**.

MODERN PRAYERS

103

For Her Majesty the Queen

Almighty Lord, of whose righteous will all things are, and were created; deepen the root of our life in everlasting righteousness. Make us equal to our high trusts, reverent in the use of freedom, just in the exercise of power, and generous in the protection of weakness.

With all thy blessings, bless thy servant Elizabeth our Queen, and all members of the Royal Family. Fill her heart and theirs with such loyalty to thee, that her people may be exalted by their loyalty to her. To our legislators and counsellors give insight and faithfulness, that our laws may clearly speak the right, and our judges purely interpret them.

May wisdom and knowledge be the stability of our times, and our deepest trust be in thee, the Lord of all Nations and King of kings; through Jesus Christ our Lord. Amen.

104

Grant, O Lord, to her Majesty the Queen
    simple faith to walk in the way set before her,
    patience and courage to bear the burden laid
    upon her,
    humility to know that her sovereignty is but
      lent by you,
    and the sure hope of eternal life with you,
    to whom belongs all dignity and greatness,
      all majesty and power,
        both in this world and in that which
          is to come.

105

Almighty God our heavenly Father, we pray thee to multiply thy heavenly gifts upon thy servant Elizabeth our Queen. Establish her throne in righteousness, uphold her continually with thy strength and guidance, and make her a blessing to the peoples over whom thou hast called her to rule; for the honour of thy Son Jesus Christ our Lord.

106

O God, who providest for thy people by thy power, and rulest over them in love: vouchsafe so to bless thy servant Elizabeth our Queen, that under her this nation may be wisely governed, and thy Church may serve thee in all godly quietness; through Jesus Christ our Lord.

107

Pour your blessing, O God, upon Elizabeth our Queen, that she may fulfil her calling as a Christian sovereign. Support her in the ceaseless round of duty, inspire her in the service of many people. Give her wise and loyal ministers; bless her in home and family; and grant that through her we her people may be knit together in one great commonwealth, a joy and strength to all its members and an instrument of your wise and loving will; through Jesus Christ our Lord. Amen.

108

O Lord our Governor, we pray for your servant Elizabeth, set over us in your providence to be our Queen.

Give her grace and wisdom to fulfil the varied duties of her calling; enrich her in the life of her family and home; and may she always be a source of strength and inspiration to her people, and promote your honour and glory; through Jesus Christ our Lord. Amen.

109

O God, the King of glory, who hast set thy servant Elizabeth, our Queen, upon the throne of her fathers: establish her, we beseech thee, in thy grace, endue her with the manifold gifts of thy Spirit, and grant that we her people may dedicate ourselves with her to thy service; through Jesus Christ our Lord.

110

A Prayer for the Queen when Journeying Abroad

Accept, O Lord, our supplication and prayer, and prosper Elizabeth our Queen in her journey, and all the days of her life; that guided ever by thy Spirit, and protected by thy power, she may walk securely in the way that leadeth to salvation. Through Jesus Christ our Lord. Amen.

111

For the Royal Family

Almighty God, Father of all mercies and giver of all grace, we ask your blessing on the members of the Royal Family as they fulfil their service among us; that both by their word and example our nation and commonwealth may be strengthened in the love of righteousness and freedom, and preserved in unity and peace; through Jesus Christ our Lord.

112

Lord God Almighty, King of Creation;
bless our Queen and all members of the Royal
   Family.
May godliness be their guidance,
may sanctity be their strength,
may peace on earth be the fruit of their labours,
and their joy in heaven thine eternal gift;
through Jesus Christ our Lord. Amen.

113

O Lord our Governor, we humbly pray thee to look with thy favour upon our country and to visit us with thy salvation. Graciously bless thy servant our Queen and every member of the royal family. Give wisdom and courage to our leaders; prosper the work of thy Church in our land; and so turn the hearts of our people to thyself that thy name may be exalted among us as our mighty God and Saviour; for the glory of thy Son Jesus Christ our Lord.

114

For the Queen and Nation

O Lord, thou God of righteousness and truth, grant to our Queen and her government, to members of parliament and all in positions of responsibility, the guidance of thy Spirit. May they never lead the nation wrongly through love of power, desire to please, or unworthy ideals, but always love righteousness and truth; so may thy kingdom be advanced and thy name be hallowed; through Jesus Christ our Lord.

115

We pray, O God, for your servant Elizabeth our
Queen, for the ministers of the Crown and all members of parliament. Guide those who rule over us and
help them to govern in your faith and fear; and enable
them so to order our national life that selfishness
and injustice may be defeated, and all may strive
together for the common good; to the praise and
honour of your name.

116

Let your mercy and blessing, O Lord of lords, rest
upon our land and nation, and upon all the powers
which you have ordained over us:
our Queen and those in authority under her,
the ministers of state,
and the great councils of the nation;
that we may lead a quiet and peaceable life in all
godliness and honesty.
Rule the hearts of our people in your faith and
fear; rebuke the power of unbelief and superstition;
and preserve to us your pure Word in its liberty
and glory even to the end of days; through Jesus
Christ our Lord. Amen.

117

We pray, O God, for your servant Elizabeth our
Queen, for the ministers of the Crown and all
members of parliament. Guide those who rule over
us and help them to govern in your faith and fear;
and enable them so to order our national life that
selfishness and injustice may be defeated, and all may
strive together for the common good; to the praise
and honour of your name. Amen.

118

Sovereign Lord of all peoples and nations, we pray
for our gracious Queen, and those who are called to
leadership among their fellows; give them vision to
see far into the issues of their time, courage to uphold
what they believe to be right, and integrity in their
words and motives; and may their service promote
welfare and peace throughout the world; through
Jesus Christ our Lord. Amen.

119

Bless our Prime Minister, O Lord, those who bear
office under the crown, and all members of Parliament, and strengthen them in their great
responsibilities.
  Put far away from them any cheap desire for

personal gain or party advantage; unite them in seeking the safety, honour, and welfare of our Queen and country.

May they not conduct their debates or reach their decisions relying upon their own frail human wisdom, but upon that which comes to all who seek to follow you and to walk in your ways, through Jesus Christ our Lord.

120

Almighty God, King of kings and Lord of lords, hear us as we pray to thee for the nation to which we belong. Guide with thy eternal wisdom our Queen and her counsellors; make us strong in faith and righteousness and in the love of freedom; and grant that we may still be counted worthy to do our part in leading the nations of the world into the paths of peace; for the honour of Jesus Christ our Lord.

121

O God, the Lord of men and nations, we remember before thee our Queen and all in authority under her who share the responsibility of government. Give them wisdom and insight, courage and high resolve, that truth and justice may inspire their counsels and govern their decisions, to the glory of thy name; through Jesus Christ our Lord.

122

For the Queen and Commonwealth

Almighty and everlasting God, who art King of kings and Lord of lords: Guide, we pray thee, the destinies of our commonwealth of nations. Direct the counsels of our Queen and all in authority under her. Strengthen the resolve of our people; deepen the sense of unity among the members of this great family; and grant us grace that we may strive manfully under thy banner for the establishment of righteousness and peace among the nations of the world; through Jesus Christ our Lord.

123

O Lord God of our fathers, who in thy goodness hast led this people hitherto by wondrous ways; who makest the nations to praise thee, and knittest them together in the unity of peace; we beseech thee to pour thine abundant blessing upon the dominions over which thou hast called thy servant Elizabeth to be Queen. Grant that all, of whatever race or tongue,

may be united in the bond of brotherhood, and in
the one fellowship of the faith; so that we may be
found a people acceptable unto thee; through Jesus
Christ our Lord.

124

We thank you, O Lord, for the Commonwealth, and
that so many millions of men and women are united
in their loyalty to the Queen and in their love of
freedom and justice.

Help us to play our part, however small it may be,
in making it an increasing force for good in the world.
Teach all who belong to it to seek first your kingdom
and righteousness, that it may become an instrument
for your purpose in the world, and its influence used
for the benefit of all mankind, through Jesus Christ
our Lord.

125

We give thanks, O Lord our God, for the peoples of
many races, languages and cultures who are bound
together with us in the British Commonwealth of
nations under our most gracious Queen.

Deepen our understanding of one another's
needs; strengthen among us the spirit of mutual

responsibility and service as members of one family; and unite us all in the cause of justice, in the love of freedom, and in the quest for peace and order; through Jesus Christ our Lord.

126

Eternal God, who rulest in the kingdoms of men: grant, we most humbly beseech thee, honour and safety to our Sovereign Lady the Queen; peace throughout the Commonwealth of her peoples; promotion of true religion, encouragement to learning and godly living; a patient service to the concord of the world; and, by all these, glory to thy holy name; for his sake to whom thou hast given all power in heaven and earth, even our Lord and Saviour Jesus Christ.

127

For the Queen's Ecclesiastical Household

O Lord our Governor,
by whose grace your servant Elizabeth
is set upon the throne as Queen:
we pray for those who are her spiritual minders,
that as they minister to her wisdom and grace
she may ever be

a source of encouragement to her Parliament,
a source of strength to her subjects,
a source of inspiration to her councils,
a source of blessing to her family,
a source of sacrificial service
to your greater honour and glory;
through Jesus Christ our Lord.

FROM SCOTTISH SOURCES

128

The Liturgy of John Knox. This book is more properly known as *The Book of Common Order 1564*. This extract is from the edition in which 'the old spelling and phraseology is strictly adhered to'.

Almightie God and heavenlie Father,
since thou hast promised to graunte our requests,
which we sal make unto thee
in the name of our Lord Jesus Christ, thy welbeloved
   Sonne . . .
we therefore, (having first thy commandement
to praye for such as thou hast appoynted rulers and
   governours over us . . .),
make our earnest supplication unto thee, our moste
   merciful God and bountiful Father,

that for Jesus Christ's sake, our onelie Saviour and
    Mediator,
it would please thee of thine infinite mercy,
freely to pardon our offences,
and in such sorte to drawe and lift up our hearts and
    affections towardes thee,
that our requestes may both procede of a ferevent
    minde,
and also be agreable unto thy most blessed wil and
    pleasure,
which is onely to be accepted.

We beseeche thee, therefore, O heavenlie Father,
as touching all princes and rulers
unto whome thou hast committed the administration
    of thy justice,
and namely as touching the excellent estate of the
    Quenes Majestie,
and all her honourable Counsel,
with the rest of the magistrates and commons of her
    realm,
that it would please thee to graunte her thine Holy
    Spirit,
and increase the same from time to time in her,
that she may with a pure faith acknowledge
Jesus Christ thine onlie Sonne, our Lord,
to be King of all kings and Governour of all
    governours,
even as thou hast given all power unto him
both in heaven and in earth;
and so give herselfe wholy to serve him,

and to advance his kingdom in her dominions
(ruling by thy worde her subjectes,
which be thy creatures, and the shepe of thy pasture),
that we being mainteined in peace and tranquillitie
bothe here and everie where,
may serve thee in all holiness and vertue;
and finally, being delivered from all feare of enemies,
may render thankes unto thee all the days of our
    life . . .

129

*A Prayer for the Queene**

O Lord Jesus Christ,
most high, most mightie King of kinges,
the onely Ruler of Princes, the very Sonne of God,
on whose right hande sitting,
doest from thy throne behald al the dwellers upon
    earth,
with most lowly hearts we beseche thee,
vouchsave with favourable regarde
to behald oure most gracious sovereigne lord, King
    James the Sixte (*sic*),*
and to replenish him with the grace of thy Holy
    Spirit,
that he alway incline to thy wil and walke in thy way;
kepe him farre of from ignorance,
but through thy gift let prudence and knowledge

alway abounde in his Royal heart;

so instruct him (O Lord Jesus), ringing upon us in earth,

that his humane Majestie alway obey thy Divine Majestie in feare and dreade:

Indue him plentifully with heavenly gifts;

graunt him in health and wealth long to live:

Heap glorie and honour upon him:

Glade him with the joye of thy countenance:

So strengthen him, that he may vanquish and over-come al his and our foes,

and be dread and feared of al the enemies of this his Realme. Amen.

* This rather quaint confusion appears without any explan-ation offered.

130

A Prayer for the Queen, probably written in 1629

Almighty God wee beseche the to blesse our gracious Queen

and endue her with thy holy Spirit,

give her to prosper with all happiness,

and mack her a happie mother of sucesfull children,

to the increase of thy glorie,

the comfort of his Majestie,

the preservation of the Churche and true religion
  amongst us,
And this life ended, grant her, O God,
to live with the in thy kingdome for ever,
through Jesus Christ our lord. Amen.

131

From *The Scotch Minister's Assistant*, 1802.

. . . More particularly, we pray, that thou wouldst
  regard with special mercy,
our highly favoured, but ungrateful nation.
Though our iniquities testify against us,
yet for thy own name's sake,
continue to us the light of the gospel,
and the means of grace that we enjoy.
Preserve us from public calamities,
and put an end to those enormities which call for
  thy vengeance upon us.
May that righteousness which exalts a nation
  flourish amongst us,
and deliver us from sin, which is the reproach and
  ruin of any people.
Bless our rulers and governors, supreme and
  subordinate.
Eminently bless and long preserve
our gracious Sovereign King George,
his Royal Consort Queen Charlotte,
the Prince and Princess of Wales, and all the Royal
  Family.

Establish our King's throne in righteousness.
Continue to inspire him with a love of Justice, a
    zeal for religion,
and a generous concern for the happiness of his
    subjects.
Defend him against the evil designs of malevolent
    and seditious men,
and give him victory over all his and the nation's
    enemies,
both at home and abroad.

132

. . . We recommend to thee our Sovereign the King,
and all the branches of His Family,
entreating thee to continue to us by their means,
the invaluable blessing of the protestant succession.
By thy grace, animate those who are distinguished
    by power, riches, or talents,
that they may improve all for the public good . . .

133

From *The Minister's Directory*, 1856.

. . . Continue thy mercies, O Lord, to this guilty
    land,
of which we are sinful members.
Bless abundantly her Majesty, the Queen,
who sways the sceptre over these realms.
Protect her person and direct her counsels,
and prosper all her endeavours for the peace and
    welfare of her dominions.
Give thy favour to her royal consort, Prince Albert,
and vouchsafe thine almighty protection to the
    Prince of Wales,
and all the members of the royal family.
Surround the Queen's throne with the wise and
    faithful of the land,
men fearing God and hating covetousness . . .

134

. . . We pray for thy servant, our Sovereign the
    Queen.
May she live long to sway the sceptre over a free, a
    loyal, and a happy people.
May her throne be surrounded by the wisest and
    best of our land,
and may all the measures which they adopt be
    rendered subservient to the public good.

We pray for our Queen's Consort, Prince Albert,
the Prince of Wales, and all the royal family.
May they be adorned with all the grace and virtues
  which become their station . . .

135

From *Prayers for Social and Family Worship*, for the use
of Soldiers, Sailors, Colonists, Sojourners in India, and
persons, at Home or Abroad, who are Deprived of the
Ordinary Services of a Christian Ministry, authorised by
the General Assembly of the Church of Scotland, 1864.

. . . O God, who hast the hearts of rulers in thy
  hands,
we beseech Thee to direct and govern all kings,
  princes, and magistrates,
to whom Thou hast committed temporal power,
so that they may ever rule in Thy fear.

Especially do we beseech Thee thus to bless our
  Sovereign Lady, Queen Victoria.
Let Thy fatherly favour ever preserve her,
and Thy Holy Spirit govern her heart;
and enable her in such wise to execute her office,
that religion may be purely maintained,
manners reformed,
and sin punished according to the Holy Word.
Bless also Albert Edward Prince of Wales, the
  Princess of Wales,

and all the other members of the Royal Family.
Plentifully bestow on them the bounties of Thy
  providence,
and yet more enrich them with the treasure of Thy
  grace . . .

136

From *United Free Church Prayers*, 1907.

. . . Watch graciously over all kings, princes and
  governments,
and hear our intercessions for them:
Put into their hearts thoughts of peace and
  concord.

We beseech Thee, especially, to pour down Thy
  blessings in a plentiful manner
upon our gracious Sovereign, Edward,
Queen Alexandria, George, Prince of Wales, the
  Princess of Wales, and all the Royal Family.
May our King enjoy a long and happy reign over
  us;
stablish him in Thy faith, fear and love,
that he may walk before Thee as Thy servant, and
  ever seek Thy honour and glory.
Bless both houses of Parliament,
and direct their counsels . . .

137

From *United Free Church Prayers*, 1909.

O God, in whose hands are the hearts of kings,
direct our Sovereign with Thy wisdom,
that all his counsels may be pleasing in Thy
   sight.

Replenish him the grace of Thy Spirit,
that he may always incline to Thy holy will;
endue him plenteously with heavenly gifts,
and grant him success in all that is good.

Preserve the Royal family amid the dangers and
   temptations
of their high estate;
in all humility and godly fear
may they serve Thee faithfully,
that they may inherit the crown of eternal life.

138

A Prayer for Empire Day

From the Church Service Society.

. . . O Lord our God, who alone rulest in the
    kingdom of men,
let Thy blessing rest continually
on our sovereign Lord, King George.
May his kingdom ever be Thy Kingdom,
Thy law his law,
Thy glory his renown.
Bless also, we beseech Thee, our gracious Queen
    Mary,
Edward Prince of Wales, and all the Royal Family.
Endue them with thy heavenly grace,
that they may adorn their high station in all
    virtuous living . . .

139

Prayers for the Queen's Silver Jubilee, 1977

From the General Assembly's Committee in Public Worship
and Aids to Devotion.

Lord God Almighty,
who didst give thy Son to be crowned with thorns
and raised him from the dead to be crowned with
    glory,

continue to grant our sovereign lady Queen Elizabeth
the blessing of faith in him and devotion to him,
that at last she may, with all thy people,
attain to the eternal Kingdom of Christ,
who liveth and reigneth with thee and the Holy Spirit,
ever one God, world without end. Amen.

140

A SERVICE IN GLASGOW CATHEDRAL, 17 MAY 1977

Eternal God,
we give thanks unto thee for thy gift to us in
    Elizabeth our Queen,
sharing the Scots heritage,
delighting in the beauty and life of our countryside
    and towns,
and fostering the well-being and happiness of us
    her people.

We bless thee for the twenty-five years wherein she
    hath reigned over us,
years in which men have climbed the highest
    mountain
and walked upon the moon;
and have sought to develop a caring society,
with greater freedom and opportunities for all.

We give thee thanks for her personal example of
    courage and responsibility,

of a happy home and of steadfast faith;
and for her concern that reconciliation should be
found
wherever it is needed among the family of
mankind . . .

141

The Blessing at the end of the service was based on that
used at the Coronation of King Charles I at Holyrood.

The Lord bless thee and keep thee;
and as he hath made thee Queen over his people,
so may he still prosper thee in this world,
and in the world to come make thee partaker of his
everlasting felicity. Amen.

142

From *The Book of Common Order of the Church of Scotland*,
1994.

Receive our prayers:
for the peace that comes from above,
and for the salvation of our souls;
for the peace of the world,
and for the welfare of the Church;
for the nations of the world

and peoples of every race;
for our Queen, our country,
and for those who bear responsibility
for the affairs of this, and every land;
for all who are in trouble,
who are poor, who are broken;
for those who love this church,
who have helped to build it up,
and especially for those who cannot be here now
but whose thoughts and prayers are with us;
for the minister and people
of this parish and congregation:
Holy God, holy and mighty, holy and immortal,
have mercy upon them
and upon all for whom we have prayed;
through Jesus Christ our Lord. Amen.

143

God of righteousness,
hear our prayer for the life of our country.
Bless the Queen
and those in positions of authority.
Bless the people:
rule their hearts and encourage
their endeavours for good.
Help us to seek service before privilege,
public prosperity before private gain,
and the honour of your name

before the popularity of our own.
Give us liberty, peace, and joy,
and bind us in service to the community
and in loyalty to you;
through Jesus Christ our Lord. Amen.

144

We pray for our nation.
Bless the Queen and the Royal Family.
Direct the Government, members of Parliament,
and all who in various ways
serve the community.
Grant that none in our land
may be despised or rejected,
and that your kingdom of love may prevail.

145

God of power and love,
bless our country and commonwealth.
Give wisdom and strength to the Queen,
govern those who make the laws,
guide those who direct our common life,
and grant that together we may fulfil our service
for the welfare of the whole people
and for your praise and glory.

146

Remember the nations of the world.
Bring to an end all war and strife:
break down the barriers of race and creed,
that all may live
as members of one family of God.
Remember our country.
Bless the Queen and her family;
and guide us in the influence we have
on our community and nation.
Preserve us as a people
from all that is degrading,
and raise us to the righteousness
of serving your will.

CURIOSITIES

147

From 'A prayer used in the Queen Majesty's house and Chapel for the prosperity of the French King and his nobility, assailed by a multitude of notorious rebels that are supported and waged by great forces of foreigns', 21 August 1590

O most mighty God, the only protector of all Kings and Kingdoms, we thy humble servants do here with one heart, and one voice, call upon thy heavenly grace, for the prosperous estate of all faithful Christian Princes, and namely at this time, that it would please thee of thy merciful goodness to protect by thy favour, and arm with thine own strength, the most Christian King, the French King, against the rebellious conspirations of his rebellious subjects, and against the mighty violence of such foreign forces, as do join themselves with these rebels, with intention not only to deprive him most unjustly of his kingdom, but finally to exercise their tyranny against our Sovereign Lady, and this her Kingdom and people, and against all other, that do profess the Gospel of thy only Son our Saviour Jesus Christ.

Now (O Lord) is the time, when thou mayest shew forth thy goodness, and make known thy power; for now are these rebels risen up against him, and have fortified themselves with strange forces, that are known to be mortal enemies both to him and us. Now do they all conspire and combine themselves against thee, O Lord, and against thy Anointed. Wherefore, now, O Lord, aid and maintain this just cause; save and deliver him, and his army of faithful subjects, from the malicious cruel bloody men: send him help from thy holy Sanctuary, and strengthen him out of Zion. O Lord, convert the hearts of his disloyal subjects, bring them to the true and due obedience of Jesus Christ. Command thy enemies not to touch him, being thy Anointed, professing thy holy gospel, and putting his trust only in thee: break asunder their bands, that conspire thus wickedly against him; for his hope is in thee: let his help be by thee: be unto him as thou wast to king David, whom thy right hand had exalted, the God of his salvation, a strong castle, a sure bulwark, a shield of defence and place of refuge.

148

A Prayer for Indian Princes, for use during the Royal visit to India, November 1911

We make our prayer to Thee, O merciful God, for all Indian Princes and Rulers within the Empire, beseeching Thee so to guide and bless them, that under them Thy people may lead peaceable lives in all godliness and honesty; through Jesus Christ our Lord. Amen.

A FINAL PRAYER

149

GOD save our gracious Queen,
Long live our noble Queen,
   God save The Queen!
Send her victorious,
Happy and glorious,
Long to reign over us,
   God save The Queen!

Thy choicest gifts in store
On her be pleased to pour,
   Long may she reign:
May she defend our laws,
And ever give us cause
To sing with heart and voice
   God save The Queen!

Nor on this land alone,
But be God's mercies known
   From shore to shore:
Lord, let the nations see
That we in unity
Should form one family
   The wide world o'er.

SOURCES OF PRAYERS

1–4	Revised English Bible (REB), OUP & CUP, 1989.
5	Apocrypha (REB).
6–7	Selina Fitzherbert Fox, ed., *A Chain of Prayer Across the Ages* (6th edn), John Murray, 1947.
8	George Appleton, ed., *The Oxford Book of Prayer*, OUP, 1985.
9	Fox, *Chain*.
10–11	Appleton, *Oxford Book*.
12	Fox, *Chain*.
13–18	Eric Milner White and G.W. Briggs, eds., *Daily Prayer*, Penguin, 1959.
19–20	W.K. Clay, ed., *Liturgies and Occasional Forms of Prayer set forth in the Reign of Queen Elizabeth*, Parker Society, 1847.
21	Fox, *Chain*.
22	Milner White and Briggs, *Daily Prayer*.
23	Fox, *Chain*.
24	Milner White and Briggs, *Daily Prayer*.
25–26	Fox, *Chain*.
27	*Daily Telegraph*, 23 September 1998, from Deborah Cassidy, *Favourite Prayers,* Continuim.
28	REB.
29	Fox, *Chain*.

30–31   Peter D. Day, *Eastern Christian Liturgies*, Irish University Press, 1972.

32   F.E. Brightman, *The Divine Liturgy*, The Faith Press, 1922.

33–36   Fox, *Chain*.

37–40   *Book of Common Prayer*.

41–42   Clay, *Liturgies*.

43–47   Annexed to the *Book of Common Prayer* by Royal warrant until 1859.

48   St Paul's Cathedral.

49–55   Annexed to the *Book of Common Prayer* at various dates.

56–58   *1928 Prayer Book* and *Alternative Service Book 1980* (copyright © The Central Board of Finance of the Church of England).

59–63   Service sheets in Westminster Abbey Library.

64   Fox, *Chain*.

65   Margaret Pawley, *Praying for People*, SPCK, 1992.

66–67   Fox, *Chain*.

68–69   P.G. Stanwood, ed., *John Cosin: A Collection of Private Devotions 1627*, OUP, 1967.

70–71   Milner White and Briggs, *Daily Prayer*.

72–74   Fox, *Chain*.

75   Frank Colquhoun, *Parish Prayers*, Hodder & Stoughton, 1967.

76–87   Fox, *Chain*.

88   *The Liturgy* of the Catholic Apostolic Church, H. J. Glaisher, 1925.

89–91   In public domain.

92–93   International Commission on English in the Liturgy.

94–102   Crown copyright.

103   St George's Chapel, Windsor Castle, *A Collection of Daily Prayers for Her Majesty The Queen, The Order of the Garter and The College of St George.*

104   Simon H. Baynes from John Conacher, *Prayers in the Church*, OUP, 1987.

105   Colquhoun, *Parish Prayers.*

106   *New Every Morning* (New edition), BBC, 1973.

107–108   St George's Windsor.

109   Frederick B. Macnutt, ed., *The Prayer Manual*, Mowbrays, 1961.

110   St George's Windsor.

111   Frank Colquhoun, *Contemporary Parish Prayers*, Hodder & Stoughton, 1975.

112   St George's Windsor.

113   Colquhoun, *Parish Prayers.*

114   *A Book of Prayers for Students* (4th edn), SCM, 1923.

115   *New Every Morning.*

116–118   St George's Windsor.

119   John Eddison in Conacher, *Prayers in the Church* (Prayer copyright © John Eddison).

120–122   Colquhoun, *Parish Prayers.*

123   Macnutt, *Prayer Manual.*

124   John Eddison, in Conacher, *Prayers.*

125   Colquhoun, *Contemporary Parish Prayers.*

126   Jeremy Taylor in Colquhoun, *Parish Prayers.*

127   W. Gerald Jones, *Prayers for the Chapel Royal in Scotland*, 1989.

128–129   *The Liturgy of John Knox*, Hamilton, Adams & Co and Thomas D. Morison.

130   George W. Sprott, ed., *Scottish Liturgies of the Reign of James Sixth*, Edmonston and Douglas, 1871.

131–132   Harry Robertson, *The Scottish Minister's Assistant*, 1802.

133–134   James Anderson, *The Minister's Directory*, Moodie and Lothian, 1856.

135   *Prayers for Social and Family Worship*, General Assembly, 1864.

136   The Church Worship Association of the United Free Church of Scotland, *Anthology of Prayers for Public Worship*, MacNiven and Wallace, 1907.

137   The Church Worship Association of the United Free Church of Scotland, *Directory and Forms of Public Worship*, MacNiven and Wallace, 1909.

138   The Church Service Society, *Order of Service for Empire Day*, William Blackwood & Sons, n.d.

139   *A Form of Service, Sunday 22nd May 1977, A Day Recognised in Scotland for Thanksgiving for Twenty-Five Years of the Queen's Reign*, General Assembly's Committee in Public Worship and Aids to Devotion, 1977.

140–141   *Glasgow Cathedral: National Service of Thanksgiving in Scotland on the Occasion of the Silver Jubilee*, HMSO, 1977.

142–146   *Book of Common Order of the Church of Scotland*, St Andrew's Press, 1994 (copyright © Panel on Worship of the Church of Scotland).

147   Clay, *Liturgies*.

148   Fox, *Chain*.

149   Verses 1 and 2 anonymous, verse 3 W. E. Hickson (1803–70), amended Westminster Abbey.

Note: Throughout the prayers, capitalisation has been followed as in the original publications. There is therefore considerable variation in style over the years.